Kempston

INTRODUCING
PEOPLE
OF THE
BIBLE
VOLUME THREE

P. 72

Also by John Phillips

Exploring Genesis
Exploring the Psalms
Exploring Proverbs
Exploring the Song of Solomon
Exploring the Book of Daniel
(by John Phillips and Jerry Vines)
Exploring the Gospels: John
Exploring Acts
Exploring Romans
Exploring Ephesians
Exploring Hebrews
Exploring Revelation

Exploring the Future
Exploring the Scriptures
Exploring the World of the Jew
Bible Explorer's Guide

Introducing People of the Bible, Volume 1
Introducing People of the Bible, Volume 2

100 Sermon Outlines from the Old Testament
100 Sermon Outlines from the New Testament
Sermon Outlines on the Psalms

Only One Life: A Biography of Stephen Olford

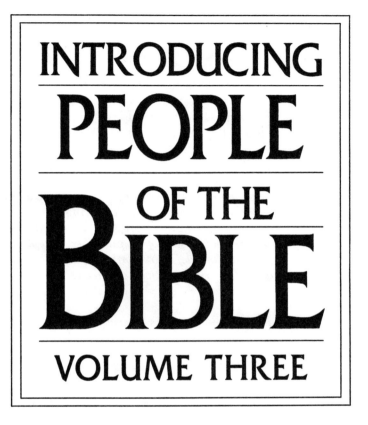

INTRODUCING
PEOPLE
OF THE
BIBLE
VOLUME THREE

JOHN PHILLIPS

LOIZEAUX
Neptune, New Jersey

INTRODUCING PEOPLE OF THE BIBLE, VOLUME 3
© *1995 by John Phillips*

A Publication of Loizeaux Brothers, Inc.,

A Nonprofit Organization Devoted to the Lord's Work
and to the Spread of His Truth

*All Scripture quotations, unless otherwise noted, are
from the King James version.*

*Library of Congress Cataloging-in-Publication Data
(Revised for vol. 3)*

*Phillips, John, 1927–
Introducing people of the Bible.
1. Bible—Biography. I. Title.
BS571.P52 1991   220.9'2   91-39819
ISBN 0-87213-629-9*

Printed in the United States of America

10 9 8 7 6 5 4 3 2 1

Contents

1
Philip
the Plodder

John 1:43-45; 6:5-7; 12:20-22; 14:8-9

I. WHAT PHILIP FOUND
II. WHAT PHILIP FIGURED
III. WHERE PHILIP FALTERED
IV. WHAT PHILIP FELT

Philip had a Greek name. The most famous Philip in Greek history was Philip of Macedon, the father of Alexander the Great. After Alexander's conquests the Greek influence was pronounced throughout the Middle East. Perhaps that is why Philip, the Lord's disciple, had a Greek name. The fact that Philip had a Greek name may have been one of the reasons Jesus chose him.

This disciple may have been named after another Philip, closer in time and territory: Philip the Tetrarch, one of the sons of Herod the Great. Philip the Tetrarch's brother Herod Philip married their niece Herodias, who afterward eloped with her husband's half brother, Herod Antipas. Herod Philip and Herodias had a daughter, Salome, who was a major player in the drama of John the Baptist's murder. Philip the Tetrarch married Salome. The Herods were a bad lot. Philip the Tetrarch was the best of them. Like his father, Philip the Tetrarch was a builder. One monument he left behind him was Caesarea Philippi at the foot of mount Hermon. He was well-liked by his subjects. Doubtless it was not at all unusual for people in those days, as in our own day, to name their sons after well-known figures such as the tetrarch.

The fact that Philip, the Lord's disciple, had this Gentile name suggests that his parents were not narrow-minded Hebrews, but more liberal-minded Hellenists. But even Hellenists would have made sure that their son had a thoroughly Jewish education.

Philip came from the city of Bethsaida, which is called by the Gospel writer "the city of Andrew and Peter" (John 1:44). Perhaps John was suggesting that these two leading men in the apostolic company were friends of Philip. (At the time Jesus was choosing His disciples, Andrew and Peter were living in Capernaum [Mark 1:21,29], but Bethsaida and Capernaum were quite close, possibly twin cities.) Not long after Andrew and Peter gave themselves to Christ, Philip did the same. Andrew had been a disciple of John the Baptist before he became a disciple of Jesus. We can imagine how Andrew would have talked enthusiastically about the Baptist and the imminent coming of Christ. No doubt Philip had been included in some of those impassioned conversations.

Philip apparently did not make much of an impact on the other disciples. If John had not rescued him from complete anonymity, all we would know about Philip would be his name and the fact that he ranks as number five in the general listing of the Lord's disciples. John told us what Philip found, what he figured, where he faltered, and what he felt.

I. WHAT PHILIP FOUND

There can be no doubt that Philip was interested in what Moses had to say about the coming of Christ. Philip knew that the Messiah was to be a kinsman-redeemer, just like Moses. "A

Prophet...like unto me" was Moses' way of describing the Messiah (Deuteronomy 18:15)! Christ would come armed with might and miracle. He would redeem Israel.

Philip, we can be sure, was at home with the glowing prophecies that spoke of the coming Son of David who would put down all His foes and reign in wisdom, love, and power. One day the desert would blossom as the rose, the lion would lie down with the lamb, a child would be able to play with a scorpion, and a man would be a mere youth at a hundred. Jerusalem would become the capital of a new world empire and the Gentiles would lay their tribute at this mighty Messiah's feet.

But Philip also knew about strange, somber, and startling prophecies that spoke of a suffering Messiah. Philip would read Isaiah 53, Psalm 22, and Psalm 69 again and again and puzzle over seeming contradictions. The Messiah was to be born in Bethlehem, yet He was to be called out of Egypt. He was to be militant, yet He was to be meek. He was to be the happy man of Psalm 1, yet He was to be the man of sorrows of Isaiah 53. Philip pondered often over the prophetic Scriptures. He may have been slow on the uptake, but he was a patient plodder. He was not the kind of man to be in a hurry to make up his mind, but he was the kind of man who arrived at a conclusion in the end. No doubt he thought, *When we finally find the Messiah, we'll see that He has fulfilled prophecy just as it's written.*

Actually Philip didn't find the Messiah, for we read that the day after Andrew brought his brother Simon to Jesus, Jesus found Philip. Philip thus became the archetype of all those people who have a personal encounter with Christ without the aid of any intermediary. They find Him by reading the Scriptures. Or they find Him simply by being found by the Lord Himself. The seeking Savior finds the seeking sinner. Jesus found Philip (John 1:43), yet Philip told Nathanael, "*We have found him,* of whom Moses in the law, and the prophets, did write, Jesus of Nazareth" (1:45, italics added). So Jesus found

Philip, and he found Jesus! The seeking sinner meets the seeking Savior.

Over and over again in the Bible we see God seeking men and men seeking God. The first question asked in the Old Testament is "Where art thou?" (Genesis 3:9) and the first question asked in the New Testament is "Where is he?" (Matthew 2:2)—a seeking Savior and a seeking sinner. There can only be one outcome: each finds the other.

"We have found him," said Philip to Nathanael! We all like to find things. We are especially pleased if what we find turns out to be valuable. We are even more pleased if we can tell other seekers that we have found what they have been looking for.

The perennial appeal of Robert Louis Stevenson's *Treasure Island* lies in the fact that the book is all about searching for buried treasure. We are intrigued with the story from the day young Jim Hawkins finds the map in the old sea captain's trunk and only narrowly escapes being killed by pirates. We follow with interest the fitting-out of the *Hispaniola* and Squire Trelawney's careless way of engaging a crew. We hold our breath when he recruits Long John Silver, the one-legged cook. We hide with Jim Hawkins in the barrel and learn of the plot by the remnant of Flint's old crew—now enlisted seamen aboard the *Hispaniola*-to seize the ship, murder the squire and the captain (and their loyal subordinates), find the treasure, and set sail for the Spanish Main.

Our interest mounts when Jim Hawkins becomes Long John Silver's prisoner and is dragged along on the pirates' final treasure hunt. "Look out for squalls," advises the squire's friend Dr. Livesey, who had given the map to the rascally cook. Our interest is sustained to the climax: the map leads the pirates to the place where the treasure was buried, but the treasure is gone! The pirates discover that their crimes have all been for nothing. Poor old Ben Gunn, marooned on the lonely island, had found the treasure and removed it long ago.

The pirates found a hole. Philip found Him! "We have

found him," said Philip and he invited his friend to come and find Him too. Those who find Him find a treasure beyond the price of buried gold and precious stones.

Philip was still trying to sort out the clues in his treasure hunt when the Lord Jesus turned the tables on him and found him instead. Philip was still poring over the old prophecies in the Word. He was still pondering about the new preacher in the wilderness. He was still searching his Bible when he found that he had been found!

II. WHAT PHILIP FIGURED

John next mentioned Philip in connection with an incident that took place near Bethsaida-Julias (not the same Bethsaida where Philip was raised) on the east bank of the Jordan river where it runs into the sea of Galilee. Jesus and His disciples had retreated to this area, which was a few hours' sail from Capernaum and an even shorter distance by land around the head of the lake.

The Passover feast was approaching and many caravans were forming as pilgrims prepared to set out on the journey to Jerusalem. Jesus could see the crowds gathering—thousands of men and an uncounted number of women and children— and His heart was moved with compassion. John the Baptist had only recently been murdered and buried, and here were all these "sheep" without a shepherd. So Jesus taught them, hour after hour throughout the day. Toward evening the disciples suggested it was time to send the crowds away. Having gathered in a desert place, the people would need to scatter to find food and lodging. "Send the multitude away," the disciples urged (Luke 9:12). "Send them away."

Philip was of the same mind as the other disciples when the Lord challenged him. "Whence shall we buy bread, that these may eat?" He asked (John 6:5). Philip was astounded. He had already been doing his homework and had arrived at an estimate of the size of the crowd—about five thousand men plus the women and the children. He had already figured how many loaves would be needed just to give each person a few mouthfuls. "Two hundred pennyworth of bread is not sufficient," he said (6:7). Perhaps that amount was the sum total of what was in the bag, or perhaps the amount was Philip's estimate of how much money would be needed. In any case two hundred pennyworth represented a considerable sum since a penny was a working man's daily wage.

The Lord had only asked Philip the question to test him and Philip failed the test. He was too much occupied with mathematics and money to be occupied with the Master. "Two hundred pennyworth of bread is not sufficient"! Those words were Philip's final offering at the altar of truth and trust. "No way!" he was saying, "not with our resources. We don't have enough money so there's no way we can feed the people."

It was a pity that Philip had not read his Bible with more attention. Had he done so he would have balked at using the number *two hundred,* for it was a number of ominous significance. The number *two hundred* is used, for instance, in connection with Achan. After the overthrow of Jericho, Achan was tempted. He knew that all the spoil of Jericho was God's first fruit and was not to be touched. Yet he stole some gold and a garment—and *two hundred* shekels of silver (Joshua 7:21). Those two hundred shekels of silver were *insufficient* to redeem his life from destruction when the day of judgment came.

The number is also used in connection with Absalom, the young rebel who sought to overthrow his father David and seize the kingdom for himself. Absalom was popular with the people, he had charm and charisma and a persuasive tongue, and he found a ready ally in the golden-tongued Ahithophel, the cleverest man in the kingdom. Moreover Absalom was handsome and his good looks were framed by a remarkable head of hair, his crown of glory. In counting up his assets Absalom did not overlook his hair—he weighed it at every year's end. "He weighed the hair of his head at *two hundred* shekels after the king's weight" (2 Samuel 14:26, italics added).

Yet that hair caused his death! When in the battle with David the tide turned against Absalom and he fled, his hair was caught in the branches of an oak—and he hung there until Joab's darts put an end to him.

The number *two hundred* is used in connection with Micah's graven image (Judges 17). First this unscrupulous man stole eleven hundred shekels of silver from his mother. Then, frightened by her curses, he gave them back to her. Then his mother took *two hundred* of those shekels and had them melted down and made into a couple of images. Next he persuaded a landless Levite to be the priest of his idol temple for an annual ten shekels, a suit, and his meals. Later the tribe of Dan persuaded the young Levite to abandon his patron, take Micah's idols, and become priest to the whole tribe. (The young Levite's name was Jonathan. He was the son of Gershom, the son of Moses. So incensed were the later Hebrew scribes with this defection of a grandson of Moses that they changed the name of the grandfather from Moses to Manasseh—to spare Moses' name and memory.) Those two hundred shekels of silver and the silver idols made from them brought disaster on the tribe of Dan. Its name is blotted out from the blessing recorded in Revelation 7.

When Ezra brought his contingent of Jews back to the promised land, he had with him *two hundred* singing men and singing women (Ezra 2:65). When they arrived back in the land and inaugurated the true worship of God, Ezra realized that his two-hundred-voice choir was *not sufficient:* the people needed to hear him read the book of the law. He "opened the book" and taught the people out of the Word of God (Nehemiah 8:1-8). Evan Roberts, the Welsh revivalist, might have learned a lesson from Ezra. The Welsh revival—impressive and far-reaching as it was—produced no long-lasting results because it was carried on the wings of song instead of being grounded on the preaching of the Word.

So Philip ought to have sensed at once that there was something wrong with his thinking when he arrived at the

ominous number *two hundred.* Unconsciously he even la-
beled the number himself as "not sufficient." "Two hundred
pennyworth of bread is *not sufficient,*" he figured. His figuring
was wrong. He figured without Christ.

III. WHERE PHILIP FALTERED

John 12:20-22 provides another glimpse of Philip. It was
three days before the Passover. The Lord had just cursed the
fig tree, thus pronouncing doom upon the nation of Israel for
its apostasy and unbelief, and we can only imagine how full of
sorrow His heart was. With His death just a few days ahead,
Jesus was in the temple teaching.

Then it was that certain Greeks approached Philip and
asked to be introduced to Jesus. These men were not Hellenists
(Greek-speaking Jews). They were Greeks who had come up
to Jerusalem for the Passover feast. In other words they were
proselytes of the Jewish religion. These Gentiles had groped
their way to the portals of Judaism and, having heard and seen
something of Jesus, realized that their Judaism was a poor
substitute for Him. We can imagine that they were awed by the
temple and by the tremendous crowds thronging Jesus. But
hearing one of the men who was evidently one of the Lord's
personal disciples being addressed by his companions as
Philip, they ventured to approach him. Here was a disciple of
Jesus who had a Greek name! Maybe he would introduce them
to Jesus.

But poor old Philip muffed it again. All sorts of doubts and
difficulties came up in his mind: *Proselytes they may be, but they
are Gentiles. When Jesus sent the twelve of us on a Messianic
mission to the tribes, He expressly told us, "Go not into the way
of the Gentiles, and into any city of the Samaritans enter ye not:
But go rather to the lost sheep of the house of Israel"* (Matthew
10:5-6). *When the Syrophenician woman besought the Lord to
heal her child, He said, "It is not meet to take the children's
bread, and to cast it unto the dogs"* (Mark 7:27).

Pondering these words of Jesus, Philip was not at all sure the Lord would want to be introduced to any Greeks, however devout they were. Philip had failed to grasp the total change in dispensations that had been ushered in by the Jewish rejection of their Christ and the subsequent cursing of the fig tree. So instead of joyfully bringing a couple of would-be converts to Christ, he gave them the cold shoulder and told them he would have to make inquires. Even then he didn't go directly to Jesus with his predicament; he went first to Andrew. It's a wonder the Greeks didn't go away in a rage (as Naaman would have done).

IV. WHAT PHILIP FELT

Finally John showed us Philip in the upper room. The last few hours had come and the Lord and His disciples were together. Jesus had washed their feet and had declared He was about to be betrayed. He had also told Peter that he was about to deny Him three times.

Then the Lord began His last heart-to-heart talk with His disciples. "I'm going home!" He told them in effect. "Let me tell you about My Father's house. It is a house of many mansions...." He saw their sad faces and the dawning of the realization that He really was going away. They would be left as orphans in the world. They could not imagine life without Him. The last three-and-a-half years had been absolutely marvelous! They thought of all the miracles they had seen and the tremendous teaching they had heard. They thought of His wisdom, His love, and His power. They thought of His goodness, His greatness, and His grace. They could not imagine life without Him.

"Let not your heart be troubled," Jesus said. "I'll be coming back. I'm only going to get things ready for you. I'm going to pave the way for you to the Father." Then it was that Philip blurted out what was in his heart: "You keep on talking about the Father. Show us the Father, and it sufficeth us. That will be sufficient." The same old calculating mind came up short once again. Before he had said, "Not sufficient." This time he said, "*That* will be sufficient." It bordered on the insulting: "You're not sufficient. Show us the Father and that will be sufficient."

It speaks volumes for the patience of our Lord Jesus that He simply took Philip's comment in His stride. The Lord's answer was sublime. John 14:9 gives us His exact words: "Have I been so long time with you, and yet hast thou not known me, Philip? he that hath seen me hath seen the Father; and how sayest thou then, Shew us the Father?"

"What you are asking for," He was saying, "is redundant. There is not one particle of difference between the Father and Me. What He is I am; what He says I say; what He does I do. If you have seen Me, you have seen Him. If I were to show you Him, I would simply be showing you Myself. Don't you realize that for the past thirty-three years I have been the visible expression of the invisible God? I am God as He is God—except that I am God manifest in flesh. Ever since I was born I have been giving people a moment-by-moment, three-dimensional, full-color, audio-visual demonstration of God." At least Philip's blundering statement gave Jesus the opportunity to explain these truths to us!

We cannot help wondering what happened to Philip. He was in the upper room on the day of Pentecost, so he too was baptized by the Spirit of God into the body of Christ. He too was endued with power from on high, so we can be sure that Philip let his light shine in some small corner of this world.

Tradition tells us he went to Scythia—part of southern Russia—and settled in Hierapolis in Phrygia. Hierapolis, a resort town attracting people from all over the Roman world, was near the great medical center at Laodicea, so Philip would not have been far from his dear friend John, who settled at Ephesus.

Thus if tradition and conjecture are true, careful and

methodical Philip helped carry the gospel tidings into Europe. He reminds us that the Lord can use ordinary, prosaic, and dull people just as He can use clever and quick-witted people.

2
Nathanael
the Guileless

John 1:45-51; 21:2

I. WHAT HE CONTENDED

II. WHAT HE CONFRONTED

   A. He Was Discerned

   B. He Was Displayed

   C. He Was Described

III. WHAT HE CONFESSED

John always called him Nathanael. The synoptic writers called him Bartholomew. *Bartholomew* is a patronymic— that is, a surname consisting of one's father's name or an ancestor's name plus a prefix or suffix. The surname Johnson, for example, is a patronymic and thus *William Johnson* means "William, son of John." So *Bartholomew* is a surname meaning "son of Tolmai." The prefixes *Ben* and *Bar* always signal patronymics; examples from the Bible include Bartimaeus, Barabbas, Ben-hadad, and Benjamin. Peter is called Simon Bar-jona because his father's name was Jonah. We do not know which ancestor is indicated by the name Bar-tolmai although we know there was a Jewish sect known as the Tholmaens, who were dedicated to the study of the Scriptures.

The name Nathanael is more familiar to us since we are acquainted with the Old Testament prophet Nathan. *Nathan* means "gift" and *El* is a name for God, so *Nathanael* means "gift of God." The choice of the name Nathanael revealed the pious hope of the boy's parents that he would indeed be the gift of God. From what we know of Nathanael's character even before he met Christ, we can be sure they were not disappointed.

Nathanael was fortunate in his choice of friends. One of his closest friends was Philip. As soon as the Lord Jesus found Philip, he rushed off to find Nathanael. Philip was brimming over with great news: "We have found him, of whom Moses in the law, and the prophets, did write, Jesus of Nazareth" (John 1:45). Probably the two friends had often pored over the Old Testament Scriptures together, searching for the many prophecies concerning the coming of Christ. They had found Moses' prophecy that the Messiah would be a prophet like him and they had read Isaiah 53, Isaiah 63, Psalm 22, Psalm 69, and Daniel 9. Then the preaching of John the Baptist had heightened their expectations.

We can imagine then that Nathanael pricked up his ears and leaped to his feet when Philip came bursting into Nathanael's hiding place under the fig tree with the momentous words, "We have found him, of whom Moses in the law, and the prophets, did write." But when Philip added, "Jesus of Nazareth, the son of Joseph," Nathanael sat back down.

I. WHAT HE CONTENDED

"Can there any good thing come out of Nazareth?" Philip exclaimed (John 1:46). Nathanael knew Nazareth. He was a native of Cana (John 21:2), which was only five miles away, and he didn't think much of Nazareth.

The sophisticated Jews of the capital didn't think much of Galilee. With more than a touch of contempt, they called the province "Galilee of the Gentiles" (see Matthew 4:15). Remote from the theological stronghold of Judea, Galilee stood astride a busy international corridor, crossed by the great military roads from the north and by ancient caravan routes from the east. "Out of Galilee ariseth no prophet," the leaders of the Sanhedrin sneered when Nicodemus ventured to put in a tentative word for Christ (John 7:52).

They were dead wrong of course. Barak the deliverer, Elon the judge, and Anna the prophetess had come from Galilee. Jonah, the only prophet to whom Jesus directly likened Himself, came from Gath-hepher, only a few miles from Nazareth itself. Elijah, Nahum, and Hosea had either come from Galilee or carried on much of their ministry there.

The sophisticated Jerusalem and Judean Jews mocked at the grammatical errors and mispronunciations common among Galileans. All Galileans were regarded as stupid yokels. The fact that the region had a mixed population of Phoenicians, Arabs, and Greeks, as well as Jews, increased the contempt in which Galilee was held by her neighbors to the south.

The Galileans themselves were scornful of Nazareth. This provincial village seems to have had some kind of unsavory reputation, but the Lord Jesus spent thirty years of His life there. He lived in deep obscurity in the most despised province of the country, in the most despised valley of that province, and in the most despised village in that valley. For thirty years he was unknown, unrecognized, and unnoticed. So very ordinary did those years seem to His contemporaries in Nazareth that when at last in their local synagogue He proclaimed Himself to be the Messiah, they tried to assassinate Him for blasphemy.

Thus it was that when Philip added the words, "Jesus of Nazareth, the son of Joseph," he punctured the balloon of rising hope his first words had begun to inflate.

Nathanael might have argued, "Let us concede that a prophet can arise out of Galilee. Jonah came from Gath-hepher, a town of Zebulun. Hosea was of the tribe of Issachar. Nahum came from Elkosh. Elijah was the Tishbite from Tishbeh in the territory of Naphtali. A prophet can arise out of Galilee—but

Nazareth? Philip, show me one passage of Scripture that links Nazareth with the Messiah!"

Philip was a wise man. He did not attempt to argue the point with his friend Nathanael. Philip did not try to change Nathanael's opinion of Nazareth. Philip simply said, "Come and see" (John 1:46). He would introduce Nathanael to Jesus and let Jesus do the rest. That is the very essence of soulwinning.

"Come and see" is what Jesus said to two disciples of John the Baptist. When they heard their master announce that Jesus was the Lamb of God, they left John the Baptist and followed Jesus. The Lord saw them following Him and asked, "What seek ye?" They replied, "Where dwellest thou?" He answered, "Come and see." The Bible says, "They came and saw where he dwelt, and abode with him that day" (John 1:35-39). The reference is to John the Beloved and Andrew. What a time they must have had! What an endless stream of questions they must have asked Him. Perhaps, as later with the travelers on the Emmaus road, He began at Moses and the prophets and "expounded unto them in all the scriptures the things concerning himself" (Luke 24:27). Whatever happened, John and Andrew abode with Him and thenceforth they were His!

"Come and see," said Philip. It did not take Nathanael long to discover that some good thing could indeed come out of Nazareth! Nothing so good had ever come out of any city in all the long ages of time. Goodness is a rare attribute that belongs essentially to God alone. It is one of the choice fruits of the Spirit. It is a pearl of great price, a gem more valuable than rubies. Nathanael found himself up against absolute goodness. He looked into a pair of eyes that, seeing right through him, stripped away all of life's comfortable little disguises. He heard a voice that spoke the truth with a gentleness and candor that left him breathless. The words he heard were undiluted and memorable. He was in the presence of a personality that was wholly unafraid and awesome and unfathomable. Nathanael was confronted by a sincerity that hurt because it made all pretense, sham, and hypocrisy wither on contact. And love, unutterable love, shone out of those all-seeing eyes and resounded through that arresting voice. Nathanael came and saw for himself.

II. WHAT HE CONFRONTED

A. He Was Discerned

Jesus said to Nathanael, "Before that Philip called thee, when thou wast under the fig tree, I saw thee" (John 1:48). Perhaps that fig tree was in Nathanael's garden. Perhaps that fig tree was in some remote unfrequented spot, a place where Nathanael liked to get away from it all. Perhaps that fig tree shaded Nathanael from the hot Syrian sun in a place where he could be alone and muse over a verse of Scripture that had caught his attention. Wherever that fig tree was, Jesus had seen him there.

Jesus' statement must have been somewhat disquieting. It was disquieting for Adam and Eve when they first discovered the truth that it is impossible to hide from God. As they cowered among the trees of the garden in their wretched aprons of fig leaves, they heard a voice calling to them, "Where art thou?" (Genesis 3:9) They knew at once it was useless to hide. That voice penetrated every nook and cranny of Eden. The eye of God stripped aside all foliage and made every hiding place bare.

It was a terrifying truth to Adam and Eve that there was no hiding place from God. It was a tender and tremendous truth to poor, unhappy, runaway Hagar. Goaded beyond endurance by Sarah's acid tongue, Hagar had fled from Sarah and Abraham and was heading for Egypt. Hagar was totally disillusioned by the behavior of these believers. By sunrise she would cross the Egyptian frontier and bury herself again in Egypt's lifestyle and religion. But God had other plans. He could not allow her to go back into the world, back into the dark, back to the demon gods of her people, carrying with her a distorted idea of Himself. The Lord revealed Himself to Hagar, spoke to her, and gave her as fresh and as real and as unique a revelation of Himself as He ever gave to Abraham. God unfolded the prophetic page before her. He gave her an exceeding great and precious promise and told her to go back to the one place on all this earth where He had put His name. "Thou God seest me," she exclaimed (Genesis 16:13).

The fact that we cannot hide from God is a terrific or a terrifying truth depending on our relationship with Him. "I saw you," Jesus said, and Nathanael wondered what He had seen. Nathanael's innermost thoughts were to be demonstrated to be an open book to the One before whom he stood.

B. He Was Displayed

It seems that Nathanael had been reading his Bible when Jesus saw him under the fig tree. The Lord now referred to Genesis 28:12, apparently the chapter and the verse Nathanael had been meditating on when His all-seeing eye was cast upon him. "Hereafter," Jesus said, "ye shall see heaven open, and the angels of God ascending and descending upon the Son of man" (John 1:51).

Genesis 28 tells us of a day in the life of Jacob. Jacob's wiles had gotten the better of him. He had double-crossed his twin brother once too often. Esau was now breathing out threatenings and slaughter, and Jacob was forced to leave home. His first encampment proved to be memorable, for that night he dreamed of a ladder, a shining stairway linking earth to Heaven. Moreover he saw the angels of God ascending and descending that ladder.

The activity of the angel hosts in Jacob's vision is significant, for they weren't descending and ascending; they were ascending and descending. They weren't coming down from Heaven to earth and going back from earth to Heaven. They were ascending to Heaven from earth and then returning to earth from Heaven. We cannot miss the meaning—they were already here; they were stationed down here.

This world is a battlefield, a planet that has been invaded from outer space by beings of great power, intelligence, and wickedness. The planet has also been invaded by countless hosts of angelic beings from the high halls of Heaven. The ranks of the holy angels include martial angels, ministering angels, and messenger angels. These beings owe their allegiance to God and they battle principalities and powers, rulers of this world's darkness, and wicked spirits in high places who owe their allegiance to Satan.

The angels of God, it seems, have a shining stairway they use, or used to use, in order to communicate with the great white throne of God. Jacob saw them ascending. Up that endless ladder they went, laden down with sad tales of wickedness and woe. What stories of injustices and tyrannies and oppressions they carried with them, what tales of hate and malice and envy and rage, what stories of war and famine and pestilence and persecution, what tales of treachery and murder and abuse! That ladder must have seemed a veritable Everest of difficulty and pain for the angels who were weighed down with amazement that Adam's race could be so callous and cruel.

Jacob also saw the angels descending. They had made their reports and received new instructions. Down they came, having taken fresh courage from the untroubled calm and confidence that radiates from the throne of God. Iniquity was just as much a mystery to the angels as to men, but the angels sensed from the peace and power emanating from God's throne that all was well. They were reassured that although God's present purposes may be inscrutable, they are perfect and peerless. So descending the stairway with confident steps, the angels came to resume their duties. What a noble and awesome vision for a runaway young man! No wonder it changed Jacob's life.

"Well, Nathanael," Jesus said in effect, "I am that ladder. I am that living link between earth and Heaven. The angels of God ascend and descend upon Me. I am the way, the truth, and the life and no one comes to the Father but by Me."

C. He Was Described

The moment Jesus set eyes on Nathanael, He said, "Behold an Israelite indeed, in whom is no guile!" (John 1:47) The word translated "guile" here is the same word used in the Septuagint version of Genesis 27:35 to convey the idea of guile or subtlety. Genesis 27 tells us of Jacob's guile.

When Jacob stole Esau's blessing and Esau pleaded, "Bless me, even me also, O my father" (Genesis 27:34), "he found no place of repentance, though he sought it carefully with tears" (Hebrews 12:17). He had bartered his birthright years before and had forfeited the blessing along with it—not that either birthright or blessing was ever really his to sell. Nevertheless, overwhelmed suddenly and too late by the immensity of what he had thrown away, Esau burst out in anguish. Isaac, now fully aware of what had really happened, put it bluntly enough to Esau: "Thy brother came with subtilty, and hath taken away thy blessing" (Genesis 27:35).

Jesus used the same word Isaac did when He described Nathanael as an Israelite in whom was no subtlety or guile. John 1:47 has frequently been paraphrased, "Behold an Israelite indeed in whom is no Jacob!"

It took God twenty years to get to the root of the Jacob-nature in the pilgrim patriarch and bring him to the place where He could change his name to Israel. Even then the old Jacob-nature often reasserted itself. Indeed it is not until we come to the closing chapters of Jacob's life that we see him living as Israel.

But standing before Jesus was an Israelite singularly free from the guile, crookedness, and subtlety of Jacob. The Lord appreciated the guilelessness of the man. True to his nature, Nathanael did not depreciate the Lord's comment with false humility, but accepted it at face value. "Whence knowest thou me?" he said (John 1:48). In other words, "How do you know so much about me?"

Nathanael was free from the double-dealing characteristic

of some of Jacob's seed. There was something inherently transparent about Nathanael. He harbored no mixed motives in his heart. He was a man who could be trusted. He scorned the use of what are commonly called the tricks of the trade. People always knew where they stood with Nathanael. The Lord Jesus recognized this rare quality at once and spoke words intended to evoke the response that demonstrated Nathanael's guilelessness.

III. WHAT HE CONFESSED

Nathanael was quick to grasp the truth. "Rabbi," he exclaimed, "thou art the Son of God; thou art the King of Israel" (John 1:49).

"The Son of God"! That identification put Him on the throne of the universe. Nathanael's statement was a startling confession of faith. Peter took years to come to a like confession. Nathanael was far ahead of the majority of the nation of Israel in his comprehension of Christ. Nicodemus, the learned and thoughtful member of the Sanhedrin, did not rise to that realization until after Calvary. When he sought his famous midnight interview with Jesus, he hailed Him as "Rabbi...a teacher come from God" (John 3:2).

When we stand at the foot of the cross, we hear another man confess Jesus to be the Son of God: the Roman centurion in charge of His execution. But that confession was wrung out of him by the sheer weight of the evidence—darkening skies, rending rocks, bursting graves, and terrors in the temple. No such physical phenomena elicited the confession from Nathanael's soul. It was evidence enough for him that Jesus had demonstrated His deity by reading him like a book.

"The King of Israel"! That identification put Him on the throne of David. For a thousand years the Hebrew people had looked for the coming of the Messiah.

The Davidic kingdom had waxed and waned and had finally been swept away by Nebuchadnezzar, and the times of the Gentiles had begun. Cyrus the Persian had eventually restored a remnant of the Jews to the promised land and hope had revived, but Ezra, Zerubbabel, and Nehemiah had presided only over a dependency. Their mandate had been to build a temple, not a palace—to raise up an altar, not a throne. The terrible sufferings of the Hebrew people during the Syro-Egyptian struggles and the coming of the monstrous Antiochus Epiphanes had hardened the clay of persistent Jewish unbelief. The sects of the Pharisees and Sadducees and the institution of the synagogue and the Sanhedrin had hardened the clay still further. Rabbinical handling of the Scriptures had caused belief in the Bible to degenerate into adherence to the sterile traditions of the elders.

Then came the voice of John the Baptist kindling new hope. And when Christ confronted Nathanael, it took him about two minutes to make up his mind: Jesus was the King of Israel. All the Messianic promises could now be fulfilled. The King had come and soon the kingdom would come!

"Thou art the Son of God," Nathanael said. Jesus countered, "Ye shall see heaven open, and the angels of God ascending and descending upon the Son of man." Jesus was indeed that ladder of Jacob's dream. As Son of God He placed His hand upon highest Heaven. As Son of man He planted His feet firmly on the earth. God manifest in flesh, He was truly God in every sense of the word and truly man in every essential of humanity apart from sin.

Nathanael was quick to recognize the Messiah, and that is about all we know of him. Really that is all we need to know. We can be sure that a man who began with such a head start finished way out ahead. At the judgment seat of Christ it will be supremely interesting to see and hear what proof Nathanael made of his ministry in after years.

3
James
the Less

Matthew 10:3

I. HIS DESIGNATION
II. HIS DISTINCTION
III. HIS DESTINATION

He is called James the Less (sometimes James the Younger) and that's about all we know of him—just a name. But that's about all we know of hundreds of people whose names appear here and there in the Bible. At least his name *occurs* in the Bible—and that's more than can be said of the pharaoh of the oppression in the days of Moses. That's more than can be said for Alexander the Great or for the philosophers and scholars of Athens. That's more than can be said for Julius Caesar. There were millions of people on earth when James responded to the call of Christ, and the vast majority lived and died and were forgotten. Yet James had his name written in the Bible five times. That's better than making *Who's Who.*

I. HIS DESIGNATION

He is designated "James the son of Alphaeus" (Matthew 10:3). Matthew is also identified as the son of Alphaeus

(Mark 2:14). If both references are to the same Alphaeus, Matthew and James were brothers and James was a Levite. The tribe of Levi was the priestly tribe. The Levites were the legal experts of the day. Thomas is also thought to have been a brother of this James.[1]

One tradition is that before responding to the call of Christ, James the Less was a Zealot. If that tradition is true, Matthew and James could have had little or nothing in common until they both met Christ. Matthew, a Roman tax collector, was a detested publican, a collaborator with Rome, and a traitor to the Jews, while James, a vehement foe of all things Roman, was determined to strike the blow that would shake off the hated shackles of the occupying power.

The name Alphaeus is the Greek form of the Hebrew name Cleophas. The Cleophas mentioned in the New Testament was the husband of that Mary who went with the mother of Jesus and other women to Calvary on the day of the crucifixion (John 19:25).

The Bible tells us nothing else about James the Less. He asked no questions and did nothing to distinguish himself as an individual. He simply marched in step with the others. He was a listener not a talker, a follower not a leader.

But James stands at the head of a long line of men and women who love the Lord and seek to live for Him quietly and inconspicuously in the daily rounds and common tasks of life. We do not know the names of the majority of those who were thrown to the lions in the days of the persecuting caesars. We do not know the names of those hewers of wood and drawers of water who built St. Paul's Cathedral or Westminster Abbey. We do not know the names of millions who down through the ages have made up the rank and file of the faith. James the Less heads the procession of the foot soldiers of the cross.

There are four lists of the twelve apostles in the New Testament. Three are in the Gospels (Matthew 10:2-4; Mark 3:16-19; Luke 6:14-16) and one is in the book of Acts (1:13,26). In each list the names are divided into three groups of four disciples. The same disciples are always grouped together and in every case each group is headed by the same apostle. The first group includes the more prominent and conspicuous apostles and is always headed by Peter. The second group includes less well-known disciples and is always headed by Philip. The third group includes the least known disciples; they are obscure except for Judas Iscariot, whose name always appears last, covered with infamy. This third group is always headed by James the Less. His place in the lists suggests that he had at least some leadership qualities.

We can also, more or less positively, infer from Scripture that James came from Capernaum. Jesus made Capernaum His headquarters during the early part of His ministry; Peter and Andrew lived there; Matthew had his customs office there; the Lord performed many of His greatest miracles there.

It is not at all unlikely that the Lord kept an eye on Matthew and James the Less for quite a while. He saw something in this obscure James that rang true and when the time came for Him to make up the list of His personal disciples, He decided that James would make an excellent apostle.

We would have chosen someone who cut a more dashing figure. We would have wanted a banker or a millionaire. We would have thought that someone like Nicodemus or Joseph of Arimathaea was better than the retiring James. But when we stand at the judgment seat of Christ, we will applaud with cheers and hosannas the Lord's choice of this man. The Lord chose him as He chose only eleven other men in all the history of this world. And the Lord made no mistakes—not even when He chose Judas Iscariot and certainly not when He chose James the Less.

II. HIS DISTINCTION

James' distinction lies in his almost complete anonymity. He is conspicuous because he was inconspicuous. He is outstanding because he is obscure. Some of the greatest forces in the universe work silently, secretly, and unseen. Silently the snowflakes fall, building barricades and stopping the march of armies. Silently the atoms whirl, their electrons rushing around their nuclei billions of times in a millionth of a second. Silently great forests grow.

In the church James the Less is the precursor of all those who have trusted Christ, who have walked humbly with their God, and who have sought to serve Him in some small corner of the harvest field. They are unknown, unsung heroes of the faith. Consider the impact of such inconspicuous men on John Wesley, Alexander Cruden, William Booth, John Knox, and John Bunyan.

Let us begin with John Wesley. The Irish historian William Lecky, who cannot be suspected of any bias toward Christianity, declared that the Wesleyan revival saved England from the blood bath of the French revolution. He went so far as to say that the religious revolution begun in England by the preaching of the Wesleys was more important than all the splendid victories won on land and sea under the British prime minister William Pitt.

Conditions in England at the time of the Wesleys were terrible almost beyond belief. The stage was decadent, the royal court reeked of licentiousness, and the church and religion were openly scorned. Infidelity and drunkenness were epidemic. In London one house in every six was a gin mill. Bands of thugs sallied forth from the taverns to commit mayhem on ordinary citizens. The priests of the Church of England were fox-hunting parsons and a converted minister was as rare as a comet. Every kind of immorality was championed by the press. It was taken for granted that Christianity was defunct—no longer even a subject for inquiry. Then John and Charles Wesley came on the scene.

But how did John Wesley come to know Christ? He had always been religious. He admitted that as a young lad he stole from his mother's purse—but he always tithed what he stole and gave some of it to the poor! He had crossed the Atlantic to be a missionary only to discover that he himself was not right with God. Returning to England, he groped in a kind of twilight zone for some time. "What have I learned?" he asked himself. "I have learned that I who went to America to convert the Indians was never myself converted."

His journal tells us that he came to Christ in the middle of a persistent and passionate quest for the truth of God. One evening he went reluctantly to a meeting of a Christian society in London where someone was reading Luther's preface to the Epistle to the Romans. About a quarter of the way through the reading, the light suddenly dawned in John Wesley's soul. The man who was destined to bring revival to England passed from death unto life. But who invited John Wesley to the meeting? And who was reading Luther's commentary? One of the church's nobodies.

John Wesley went on to write 118 books and articles. He and his brother Charles published 49 books of hymns and poetry. John traveled some 250,000 miles, mostly on horseback, preached 40,000 sermons, and led countless thousands to Christ. But who led *him* to Christ? It was one of the fellowship of James the Less.

Think also of Alexander Cruden, born in Aberdeen on May 31, 1701. He was known as Crazy Cruden since on several occasions he displayed evidence of mental instability. He became first secretary to the earl of Derby and later he worked as a tutor. Cruden saved his money and in 1732 he rented a shop in London just a stone's throw from the royal exchange and went into the bookselling business. Shortly after he moved into the shop, he began work on the project that made him famous: the compilation of a concordance of the Bible. There is no way we can estimate how helpful that concordance has been to the cause of Christ. Anyone knowing just one word in any Bible verse can find that verse with a *Cruden's Concordance,* a work still being published more than two hundred years after its completion.

Today there are other more sophisticated concordances.

Lexicons, word studies, and computer programs undreamed of in Cruden's day are available to us. Yet in his day and for generations afterward, armies of Bible students rose up to call Crazy Cruden blessed. But who led Alexander Cruden to Christ? Nobody knows. It was a member of the fellowship of James the Less.

Another member of that fellowship had an impact on the man who became known as General Booth. Called "the prophet to the poor," William Booth was born among the poor in Nottingham on April 10, 1829. He was born again at the age of fifteen. He launched his new mission in 1865 and called it The Salvation Army in 1878.

In Booth's day London's East End was a squalid slum of half a million people. There were gin shops on every corner and some of the shops even had steps up to the counter so that the smallest child could be served. Booth took the East End by storm. Uniformed Salvationists formed brass bands and marched through the streets, and thousands of people were saved. These militant Christians stirred up fierce opposition throughout Britain. The mayor of one English city advised the people to take the Salvation Army flag, tie it around the necks of the Salvationists, and hang them with it. In the early 1880s tavern keepers, enraged because so many of their customers were getting saved and giving up drink, urged people to attack Salvation Army soldiers in the streets. When William and Catherine Booth visited Sheffield in 1882, they were attacked by a gang of toughs. General Booth, surveying his troops covered with mud and blood and egg yolks, said, "Now is the time to have your photograph taken." In one year nearly seven hundred Salvationists were assaulted on the streets of Britain simply for preaching the gospel. Some were even punched and kicked to death.

Booth's army went after the poor and the wretched. It was designed, the founder said, for "wife-beaters, cheats and bullies, prostitutes and thieves." C. H. Spurgeon said, "If the Salvation Army were wiped out of London 5,000 extra policemen could not fill its place in the repression of crime and disorder."

General Booth died (or as his fellow soldiers would say, "He was promoted to Glory") on August 12, 1912. During his lying-in-state 150,000 people filed past his coffin and 40,000 people, including Queen Mary, wife of King George V, attended his funeral. In Booth's lifetime The Salvation Army had grown to include 15,945 officers serving in 58 countries.

But who led William Booth to Christ? Some biographers say that his conversion took place in Nottingham when the revivalist Isaac Marsden was conducting a campaign. Others say Booth was converted in a small prayer meeting. Nobody knows for sure. The person who led William Booth to Christ is another member of the fellowship of James the Less.

Consider next the case of John Knox. When George Wishart was burned at the stake as a heretic, his colleague John Knox escaped arrest but he watched his mentor die. Knox saw him being led to the stake by the executioner and heard about the words of forgiveness Wishart spoke to the man. Knox watched the flames leap up around Wishart as he ascended the ladder of martyrdom to his heavenly home. That martyr made a deep and a lasting impression on Knox.

In 1547 John Knox himself was arrested and sent to France where he was condemned to be a galley slave for nineteen months. While toiling at the oars of a French galley, he showed the stuff of which he was made by boldly defying the ship's Roman Catholic chaplain who tried to intimidate him.

When John Knox returned to Scotland from his enforced exile, he began to preach. He bluntly declared the mass to be idolatry and boldly stated that Catholic churches and monasteries should be closed. He lived to see Protestantism established as the national religion of Scotland. When Mary Stuart came to the throne in 1560, she promptly had John Knox arrested and tried for treason, but the court acquitted him. The triumph of the Scottish Reformation was complete. Thomas

Carlyle, the famous Scottish essayist and historian, said that in the history of Scotland he could only find one epoch: the Reformation wrought by John Knox. Carlyle described it as "a resurrection from the dead" for Scotland.

John Knox went to his rest in 1572, but his soul goes marching on. And who led him to Christ? We know that he was profoundly moved by Wishart, but who took the Bible and pointed John Knox to Calvary? It was another member of the fellowship of James the Less.

We might also ask about the conversion of John Bunyan. He's not so well-known today, but for three hundred years he was the best-known, best-loved, most-read author in the Christian world. His *Pilgrim's Progress* stood side by side with the Bible in almost every Christian home. He was born in Bedford, England, in 1628. Just a humble tinker by trade, he was arrested in 1660 for preaching without the permission of the established church. He remained in the Bedford jail for nearly thirteen years during which his wife, his little blind daughter, and his other children suffered much. He was in jail when the terrible bubonic plague ravaged England and he was there when the great fire of London reduced much of the city to smoking ashes and rubble.

The devil could lock Bunyan up, but he couldn't shut him up! During his incarceration he wrote his famous allegory of the Christian life. "As I walked through the wilderness of this world," he began, "I lighted on a certain place where was a Den, and I laid me down in that place to sleep; and, as I slept, I dreamed a dream..." The den was Bedford jail. The dream became *Pilgrim's Progress* with its host of colorful characters who have delighted Christians from that day to this. How can we ever forget Mr. Obstinate and Mr. Pliable, or Christian in the Slough of Despond, or Mr. Worldly Wiseman and Madam Bubble, or the man with the muck rake in his hand, or Mr. Hypocrisy, or Mr. Formalist, or Mr. Mistrust, or Giant Despair? And who can forget the Delectable Mountains, the Interpreter's house, Doubting Castle, Bypass Meadow, and Vanity Fair? To spend an hour or two with John Bunyan is to be thoroughly entertained and greatly helped on the straight and narrow way that leads to life. Who can measure the power, influence, and impact of a book?

For a long time before his conversion John Bunyan was tormented by his sin. He felt as though the sun in the sky begrudged the light it gave him. He felt as though the cobblestones of the street and the tiles on the houses banded together against him. Who led him out of this darkness into light? Bunyan mentioned being associated with a Master Gifford. He also mentioned overhearing a cluster of poor women discussing the kingdom of God as they sat in the sun outside their doors, and he mentioned being influenced by the members of the little church at Bedford. But who led him to Christ and thus gave the world *Pilgrim's Progress, The Holy War,* and *Grace Abounding to the Chief of Sinners?* We'll have to wait for the answer, for it was a member of the fellowship of James the Less.

James the Less stands in the forefront of a multitude that no man can number—anonymous men and women and boys and girls who are washed in the blood of the Lamb and whose names are written down in glory. They may stand as silent sentinels on earth, but they will be numbered among the aristocracy of Heaven. No bright lights shine on their names down here, but they will shine as the stars in the firmament forever over there.

III. HIS DESTINATION

One of these days the trumpet will sound. "The dead in Christ shall rise first: Then we which are alive and remain shall be caught up together with them in the clouds, to meet the Lord in the air" (1 Thessalonians 4:16-17). We will all be there, small and great—those who made a mighty mark for God and are mentioned in church history books, and little old ladies and shy retiring men who loved the Lord and like Mary of Bethany did what they could. Those who had the gifts of apostle and prophet, evangelists and pastors and teachers who filled great pulpits, those who blazed gospel trails into dark continents, and those who founded missions and movements will rise together with countless ordinary folk toward the sky.

We will all arrive at the celestial city. Before us will be the vast bulk of that city foursquare. We will see its jasper walls stretching far away on either side and soaring upward mile after mile until they are lost in the sky above. Our eyes will be drawn to the great foundations of that wondrous city, the city that haunted Abraham's dreams. He looked for "a city which hath foundations" (Hebrews 11:10) and here he will find a city with twelve foundations ablaze with precious stones. Twelve names are engraved on those foundations for all the universe to see. And just as prominent as the names of Peter, James, and John is the name of James the Less.

We will all go on in and stand at the judgment seat of Christ. The books will be opened. The name of James the Less will be called, and we will hear what he did and where he went and what he said and whom he won to Christ. James the Less will be James the Less no more! All those of his unsung fellowship will stand with him, honored and applauded "in the crowning day that's coming by and by."[2]

---

1. The family ties among the twelve disciples can become very confusing—mostly because opinions of commentators vary. W. Graham Scroggie stated his interpretation as follows: "Most of [the disciples] were closely related to Jesus or to one another. There were two pairs of brothers, Peter and Andrew, James and John. Tradition says that Thomas, Matthew and James of Alphaeus were brothers. Jude was either brother or son of James of Alphaeus, so that, perhaps, a father and a son were in that chosen circle. And James and John of Zebedee, Thomas, Matthew, and James of Alphaeus were first cousins of our Lord, and Jude was a first cousin once removed; so that the Twelve and their Master were a family group." (*The Gospel of Mark,* Grand Rapids: Zondervan, 1979, page 65.).

2. Quotation is taken from D. W. Whittle's hymn, "The Crowning Day."

4
James,
the Son of Zebedee

Matthew 4:21; 17:1; 20:20; Mark 1:19; 5:37; 13:3; 14:33;
Acts 12:2

I. HIS FAMILY
II. HIS FAITH
III. HIS FIDELITY
IV. HIS FAME

I remember once being at sea on a troopship. Standing on the deck I could see in the distance the gray horizon where the tossing waves met the lowering sky. There was another ship out there. From time to time, riding an especially high wave, she would lift her masts above the skyline. Then she would sink back out of sight again. Such a ship, in such a sea, was the apostle James, who was the brother of John and the son of Zebedee and Salome. Once in a while we catch a fleeting glimpse of James in Scripture, but most of the time he is out of sight. We know he is there (usually when John or Peter is there); we catch the occasional glimpse of James, but most often we don't see him at all.

No I. HIS FAMILY *Disparagen*

James' father was Zebedee. Even more elusive than his son, Zebedee is seen on only one occasion in the Gospels

(Matthew 4:21-22; Mark 1:19-20). He lived at or near Bethsaida on the western shore of the sea of Galilee, where Peter and Andrew were raised. The place, often frequented by Jesus, was probably not far from Capernaum, where the Lord eventually had His headquarters during His Galilean ministry. Later on the Lord denounced Bethsaida for not receiving His teachings.

Zebedee was a successful fisherman who owned his own boats and paid other men to work for him. He was the kind of employer who keeps a watchful eye on his business. His two sons were in business with him, and there seems to have been some kind of partnership between them and Simon Peter and Andrew.

Zebedee probably had a house in Jerusalem too and was acquainted with the high priest Caiaphas and his household (John 18:15-16). We can gather that Zebedee moved in the upper social circles.

We do not know anything about his personal relationship with the Lord Jesus. Zebedee does not seem to have done anything to hinder his two sons from giving up the fishing business to become disciples of the young prophet from Nazareth. Doubtless he had hoped that his boys would continue in his fishing business and carry it on after he retired. Still he allowed them to go with Jesus and put no obstacles in their way. Some have criticized him for not going with them, but perhaps he thought it better to stay home and run the business so that he could contribute to their support.

It speaks well of a father when his boys want to follow in his footsteps. It also speaks well of a father when he unselfishly gives his sons to the Lord's work. Zebedee was a fine, hardworking man and a good father.

Salome, the mother of James, seems to have been a somewhat pushy, ambitious woman who wanted the best for her boys. We do not know how she reacted when her boys abandoned their future in the family business to trek up and down the countryside with the preacher from Nazareth. The early popularity of Jesus and His extraordinary miracles probably reconciled her to the decision her sons had made. Then when it dawned on Salome that Jesus was claiming to be Israel's rightful King, she was enthusiastically in favor of their choice.

In fact she attempted to push her sons forward in the anticipated kingdom (Matthew 20:20-28). Unknown to her, the Lord was actually on His way to Calvary when she made her move. She asked Him to give them the two highest and most important positions in His realm. We are not told what the two brothers thought of her behavior. Perhaps they were embarrassed. We do know what the other disciples thought. They were angry. In any case, the Lord denied her request.

It is possible that Salome was the sister of Mary, the Lord's mother. So perhaps Salome was trying to take unfair advantage of her family relationship. If on the purely human level Zebedee and Salome were indeed the Lord's uncle and aunt, they would have known Him from His infancy.

The circumstances of His birth were remarkable enough to have occasioned a considerable amount of gossip in the area. The character of the youthful Lord Jesus would also have been the likely subject of many conversations. He was never known to have said an unkind word or done an unkind deed. Luke said that He grew "in favour with God and man" (Luke 2:52).

Jesus was known in the area for His genius. He was a first-class scholar and a devoted student of the Scriptures. He carefully kept the letter and spirit of the Mosaic law, which He knew by heart. Stories must have been circulated about His encounter with the Jewish rabbis in Jerusalem when He was a lad of twelve.

For years the Lord labored at the carpenter's bench in Nazareth. Nobody ever had reason to complain about His workmanship. Nobody ever regretted doing business with Him. He was a craftsman whose creations were faultless. He was good and clever and kind. Nobody had a bad word to say about Him.

Doubtless He was a frequent visitor in Zebedee's home

during the thirty silent years, of which we know so little and of which we should like to know so much. So perhaps Zebedee and Salome were not at all surprised when Jesus quit the carpenter's shop and announced Himself to be the Messiah. They, of all people, would have known the truth about His birth and lineage.

Salome became an early and enthusiastic supporter of Jesus. She believed in His kingship (Matthew 20:20). She was one of the women who ministered to Him of her own substance (Luke 8:3; Mark 15:40-41). She followed Him on His last journey to Jerusalem. She was at the cross and witnessed His final suffering. She was one of the women who came first to the tomb to complete the embalming of His body. Remembering her devotion to Jesus, we can forgive her for being a bit pushy.

Salome and Zebedee's sons, James and John—the Lord's cousins—would have amazing stories and countless unrecorded details to tell on their occasional visits home. Zebedee would sit in his easy chair and listen to it all. Salome would burst out with one exclamation after another.

Of the two brothers, James seems to have been the older. Apparently it never occurred to James to be envious because his younger brother was closer to Jesus than he was. Maybe James recognized the unusual talents of his young brother who went on to write five books of the New Testament. James and John had something in common: they both loved the Lord Jesus with an ever-growing love that would unite them in everlasting bonds far more enduring than any earthly ties.

II. HIS FAITH

Reference is made to James in connection with the healing of Peter's mother-in-law, for it was right after that incident he responded to the call of Christ to become one of His personal disciples. In time James, his brother John, and his fishing partner Simon Peter formed a special inner circle among the disciples. As part of that inner circle, James was chosen by Jesus to be present on at least three significant occasions when his faith was greatly strengthened.

For instance James was in the house of Jairus, the ruler of the Capernaum synagogue, when Jesus had His first ministerial face-to-face confrontation with death. That day James saw something no one had seen for hundreds of years. Not since the days of the prophets Elijah and Elisha had anyone seen a person raised from the dead.

The daughter of Jairus had died and James saw the grief of the heartbroken parents. He witnessed the struggle in the soul of Jairus as he hoped against hope and battled so bravely with his understandable unbelief. Then James watched Jesus put out the professional mourners and turn His back on their mockery. James, John, and Peter, along with the stricken mom and dad, went into the child's bedroom. They looked at the once-fresh face of the twelve-year-old girl now cold and fixed in death. They saw Jesus take the little girl's dead hand in His and heard Him say, "Damsel, I say unto thee, arise" (Mark 5:41). They watched the blush return to her cheeks as she came back to life. James would never forget what he saw that day. He saw *the Lord's greatness*. It robbed death of all its terrors.

Later on James saw Jesus raise the widow's son and Lazarus, whose body was already rotting in the grave! No wonder James was such martyr material. He knew Jesus had conquered death and all its powers.

James was also with Jesus on the mount of transfiguration. Once more in the company of Peter and John, he walked with Jesus into the Anti-Lebanon mountains and climbed to the snow line of mount Hermon. There he saw the Lord's appearance change. James caught a glimpse of man as God intended man to be—inhabited by God and robed in a glory not of this world. Dazzled by the blazing whiteness of the Lord's home-spun robe, James saw His face shine like the sun. James saw Moses and Elijah and heard their conversation with Jesus. James heard them talk of the Lord's "decease which he should accomplish at Jerusalem" (Luke 9:31). James heard Peter's blundering words as well as the voice from Heaven. The Lord enjoined silence about the transfiguration, but James would never forget what he saw. He saw *the Lord's glory*.

Then James was with the Lord in dark Gethsemane. He heard the Lord say that His soul was "exceeding sorrowful, even unto death" (Matthew 26:38). Doubtless the mind of James was in a whirl. He had just come from the upper room where the Lord had talked more bluntly than ever before about His impending departure. James had partaken of the emblems of a new feast of remembrance, the significance of which was wholly beyond his comprehension at the time. He was bewildered by the talk of the Lord's body being broken and His blood being shed.

In the garden James promised the Lord that he would stay awake and watch and pray, but he promptly fell asleep. He was ashamed of himself, but he kept on falling asleep just the same. Jesus excused him and John and Peter so graciously: "The spirit indeed is willing, but the flesh is weak" (Matthew 26:41). But James saw the Lord's face drawn with anguish and stained with tears. He saw *the Lord's grief*.

James was with Jesus when Judas arrived with the rabble, the rulers, and the Romans. Like the other disciples, James ran away. Salome went to Calvary, but we have no intimation that James was there. John was there and the Lord consigned the future care of His mother to him, but there's no hint that James was there. If fear kept him away, he must have severely reproached himself for his desertion—until Pentecost changed everything forever.

James was in the upper room when the Lord appeared to the disciples after His resurrection. We can be sure he made up his mind then never to play the coward again. It was small comfort that the others had run away too. It was small comfort that he had not betrayed the Lord as Judas did or denied the Lord with fisherman's oaths as Peter did. It was great comfort that the Lord had forgiven him. James had learned his lesson and learned it well. He was determined that next time he found himself in a place of danger because of his confession of Christ, he would play the man. To that end he schooled his heart and mind and soul and will.

III. HIS FIDELITY

We see the fidelity of James in an incident that took place shortly after the transfiguration. Jesus had deliberately set His face toward Jerusalem and each step was bringing Him closer to the cross. His way led through Samaria. Hard feelings had existed between the Jews and Samaritans for centuries, and the city of Jerusalem stirred the religious envy of the Samaritans. When the Lord entered the province of Samaria He pointedly bypassed their holy mountain Gerizim, thus making it evident that He was on His way to Jerusalem. So when the Lord and His disciples passed through a small Samaritan village, they encountered a hostile crowd. Perhaps the Samaritans felt that Jesus had snubbed their holy site. Perhaps they resented a band of Jews taking a shortcut through their village. For one reason or another the Samaritans gave the Lord and His disciples an uncongenial reception.

James and John reacted at once. They had just seen Elijah on the mount of transfiguration—if Elijah could call down fire, they could do it too. "Lord," said James and John, "wilt thou that we command fire to come down from heaven, and consume them?" (Luke 9:54)

The call for fire was indeed appropriate: not penal fire, but Pentecostal fire! Not the fire of God's wrath, but the fire of God's grace! James and John did not yet know of what Spirit they were. They would understand better by and by.

In the meantime the Lord gave them a nickname. He called the pair *Boanerges,* "sons of thunder" (Mark 3:17). Some think that the designation was given to James and John earlier because of their hot tempers, but in any case the term comes to mind in connection with this incident.

They *were* hotheads, but they were loyal hotheads. If their zeal was mistaken, they meant well. They could not bear to see their beloved Master slighted—and by Samaritans of all people! However blameworthy James may have been at the time, the incident certainly gives us a glimpse of his fidelity.

We see another glimpse of James shortly before Calvary. The disciples were exclaiming over the wonders of the temple and the great stones in its foundation when Jesus at once foretold the impending destruction of the temple and the city. Mark 13:3-4 tells us that James was one of those who asked the Lord for more details regarding the prediction. James wanted his faith and fidelity to be intelligent and informed. In answer to James' question, the Lord picked up the threads of Old Testament prophecy and the threads of New Testament prophecy and wove them into the wondrous tapestry of His great Olivet discourse. We might say even at this belated date, "Thank you, James, for being so thoughtful as to ask that question."

Then in the last chapter of the Gospel of John we see James on the seashore after the Lord's resurrection. The Lord had promised to meet the disciples in Galilee, so off to Galilee they went, back to the towns and villages and scenes and memories of their earlier years. Before long Peter got tired of waiting for Jesus and announced that he was going back to fishing. James was one of the other six disciples who fell in step with Peter. Down to the shore they went, just like old times. It was as though nothing had ever happened and that the three years they had spent with Jesus were all a lovely but impossible dream. The familiar boat, the ropes, the sails, and the nets were still there. The disciples launched out into the water, let down the nets, and toiled all night. The result was—nothing! They had come back to nothing! Then Jesus came and told them what to do and called them afresh to His work.

Like the others, James sat there shamefaced enough and, in uneasy silence, ate the breakfast the Lord provided. He listened as the Lord dealt with Peter. James heard Him silence

Peter when he wanted to know what John's future would be. James heard the Lord's veiled but unmistakable prophesy of the terrible death Peter would die. And James made up his mind: he too would die, if need be, for the One who had died for him.

IV. HIS FAME

Around A.D. 44 James was murdered by Herod Agrippa I. The church was just ten years old. The Herods were a cruel and dangerous family. Three or four of them come into the gospel story and a quick glance at them will be useful.

Herod the Great, as the world calls him, was the man who murdered the babes of Bethlehem in an attempt to get rid of the infant Christ. He was an Edomite sitting on the throne of David and lording it over the people of God. He was such a brutal tyrant that even his own family was not safe. He had nine or ten wives and not only murdered his favorite, but also murdered her two brothers and some of his sons as well. Just five days before he himself died, he ordered the death of his son Antipater. No wonder the emperor Augustus said it would be better to be one of Herod's hogs than one of his sons! When Herod knew his life would soon be over, he rounded up all the leading Jews and gave orders for them to be massacred the day he died. "The Jews will not mourn me," he raved, "but they will mourn." Toward the end of his life he suffered terribly. A horribly painful and foul disease seized him and his agony was indescribable. His sores stank so badly that people dreaded having to be in his presence.

Then there was Herod Antipas, the son of Herod the Great. Antipas had a reputation for craftiness and cunning, and one historian called him "a wily sneak." He stole his half brother Herod Philip's wife Herodias, and she in turn goaded Antipas on to murder John the Baptist. That crime so haunted his conscience that he grew superstitious about Jesus, especially as the reports of His miracles circulated throughout the country.

Herod Antipas secretly hoped someday to witness a miracle. He thought his time had come when Pilate, finding that the trial of Jesus was likely to be a very dangerous business indeed, sent Jesus to Herod Antipas for judgment. Antipas was delighted, thinking now he would see a miracle. However, Jesus simply ignored him until at last Antipas, enraged by the Lord's silence, mocked Him and poured scorn on His claim to be King. So this Herod began by murdering John the Baptist and ended by mocking Jesus.

Herod Antipas was succeeded by Herod Agrippa I, a grandson of Herod the Great. The Herods had the confusing and unhealthy habit of marrying each other. Herod Agrippa I, for instance, was the child of two first cousins. He married another cousin who was the daughter of his aunt who was married to an uncle! Agrippa was a close friend of Caligula, one of the maddest of the caesars. Agrippa was the Herod who murdered James in an attempt to curry favor with the Jews. Later he accepted divine honors for himself and died under the stroke of God.

James was the first of the apostles to suffer martyrdom. One tradition is that before his martyrdom James went to Spain to preach to Jewish captives in exile there. Herod Agrippa I had sent the Jews to Spain as slaves, so if James did indeed go there to minister to them, Agrippa would have thought he had sufficient grounds for executing him. The execution of James pleased the Jews so much that Agrippa, wanting to humor his difficult subjects, went on to arrest Peter.

It is one of the mysteries of God's providence that Peter escaped and James was martyred. But it was only a decade or two before Peter was martyred also. Doubtless Peter was welcomed to his new home in Heaven by both Jesus and his old fishing partner James. James, through his mother, had once made a bid for a crown. Now he wears a martyr's crown in a land of fadeless day where he sits enthroned as one of the mighty apostles of the Lamb.

5
Matthew, the Tax Collector

Matthew 9:9-13; Mark 2:14-17; Luke 5:27-32

I. HIS MONEY

II. HIS MASTER

III. HIS MANUSCRIPT

    A. The King Is Revealed

        1. His Person

           a. His Ancestry

           b. His Advent

           c. His Ambassador

           d. His Adversary

        2. His Purpose

           a. His Men

           b. His Mandate

        3. His Power

    B. The King Is Resisted

    C. The King Is Rejected

    D. The King Is Raised

Matthew is called "the son of Alphaeus" (Mark 2:14). So is James the Less, but it is possible that Matthew's father was not the same Alphaeus who was the father of James the Less. Matthew's name is usually linked with that of Thomas and it is not at all unlikely that they were brothers. Thomas is called *Didymus,* which means "the twin," so perhaps he and Matthew were twin brothers. Some scholars think that Thomas, Matthew, and James the Less were brothers.

There were several sets of brothers in the apostolic fellowship. Andrew and Simon Peter were brothers. James and John were brothers (since their mother Salome is thought to have been the sister of Mary, the Lord's mother, James and John may also have been the Lord's cousins). James the Less and Jude (Judas) may have been brothers. Half the company of the disciples was made up of pairs of brothers.[1]

Matthew always referred to himself as Matthew. Mark and Luke always referred to him as Levi. We usually think of Matthew first as a tax collector.

I. HIS MONEY

At one time Matthew had plenty of money. The trouble was that his money had been treasured up at the price of infamy, for he was a publican, a tax collector for the Roman government. Most Jews branded him an outcast, for they considered the publicans to be traitors in the pay of the detested occupying foreign power.

Moreover tax collectors were not at all scrupulous about how they amassed their private fortunes. They used the system to their own advantage. Roman officials farmed out the actual job of collecting taxes and gave each collector a quota. What he collected over and above the quota was his to keep. As a result extortion was common and the tax collectors preyed on rich and poor alike.

Matthew had an office in Capernaum, a busy town on the northwest shore of the sea of Galilee. There he collected taxes from the fishermen and from the caravans that came that way. We do not know how he came to be so employed. His choice of a profession must have broken his parents' hearts, for he was born a Levite.

To be born a Levite was considered a privilege, for that family was set apart by God for the handling of holy things. Children of the Levites were well-grounded in the Scriptures. Matthew's familiarity with the Old Testament is evident throughout his Gospel. The Levites were the experts in Mosaic law and rabbinic traditions.

Their tribal history was unique. Every other tribe was given a province of its own, but the tribe of Levi had no such territorial holding. Instead it was given a number of cities (including six "cities of refuge") scattered throughout the territories of the other tribes. Thus the Levitical tribe was supposed to have a godly, leavening influence on the more secular tribes. The Levites were denied property in this world so that they might lay up treasure in Heaven. The Levitical tribe derived its income from the tithes and offerings of the other tribes.

Young Matthew seems to have taken a dim view of this arrangement. We can imagine that when his mother asked him what he wanted to be when he grew up, he did not say he wanted to be a Levite. When she said, "What are you going to be?" he replied, "Rich!" The Levitical system of living on handouts from other Israelites was not for him. Matthew was sick of that kind of life. He intended, when he grew up, to get rich as fast as he could. When in his bed at night or in his wanderings here and there he thought about how to get rich quick, one sure-fire way became obvious. He would become a tax collector.

Why not? he reasoned. *I might as well accept the situation as it is. The country is occupied by Rome and that is a fact of life not likely to change in my lifetime. So what if tax collectors are despised and classified with harlots and sinners? I don't need to be an extortioner. I will just make a fair commission. My parents are wedded to the old ways, trying to earn a living teaching the Mosaic law. But surely the only law that really matters is Roman law. I cannot spend the rest of my life tied to my parents' apron strings. I'm sorry they will be upset by my decision, but it's my life after all. I'm going to become a tax collector.*

To that end Matthew gave attention to his education so that he would be literate and at home in both the Jewish and Roman worlds and able to handle basic math and bookkeeping. And eventually he became a publican and joined a small tightknit community of rich social and spiritual outcasts. He shrugged off the vision of his parents' anguished faces and their shame and went about the business of making money.

Matthew probably knew Zebedee and his sons quite well. They were prosperous fishermen and doubtless paid their taxes to him. So did Jonas and his boys Andrew and Peter.

Very likely Matthew saw Jesus when He visited the area. Probably he knew His reputation for integrity, workmanship, generosity, and plain old-fashioned goodness even before Jesus gave up the carpentry business in Nazareth, went down to Jordan to be baptized of John, and then reappeared as a preacher and miracle worker. Perhaps Jesus showed His scorn of gossip and cutting public opinion by occasionally stopping to pass the time of day with Matthew.

II. HIS MASTER

It is unlikely that Matthew was really a happy man. He may have laughed and joked when he was with his own company—that tight little circle of tax collectors who shrugged off the scorn of their fellows by throwing lavish parties for each other and hiring entertainers of questionable morals and few scruples. But the snubs and sneers of the Jews, his excommunication from temple and synagogue, and the pained stricken looks on the faces of his parents must have cut deeply into Matthew's soul. Perhaps he had already discovered that money—lots and lots of money—couldn't make a man happy.

Then one day, like a bolt out of the blue, a voice of authority and command offered the opportunity of a lifetime. There was Jesus of Nazareth hailing him, and there was a handful of His new disciples. The disciples were looking him over with very mixed feelings indeed, but the Master was looking into his very soul. The disciples saw the publican; Jesus saw the person. Jesus saw the man beneath the empty mask of indifference and bravado. "Follow me," He said. That was all. It was enough. Matthew did not hesitate for a moment. He handed his account book over to his assistant, appointed a successor, and then walked out of the tax-collecting business forever. Matthew was a changed man.

Perhaps the Master's call came to him as an unexpected challenge. Perhaps he had been thinking about a change for a long time. Perhaps he had heard some of Jesus' sermons, seen some of His miracles, and talked to Him privately at night like Nicodemus. Perhaps Matthew had been longing and yearning for just such a call. In any case, it did not take him long to make up his mind. He didn't say, "I'll think it over." He rose up and followed Jesus.

We can believe that Matthew's decision caused quite a stir in and around Capernaum. The gossip spread from village to village: "Guess what! Jesus of Nazareth has a new disciple—a publican. He must be hard up for disciples."

But Jesus wanted Matthew. He wanted him for Himself—He saw beneath the surface to the sound quality of the man. But He also wanted the skills that Matthew had. They would be invaluable later on in establishing His kingdom in the hearts and lives of men. He wanted the businessman in Matthew.

Most of the Lord's disciples were only average people. Judas was the only Judean; the rest were Galileans and the Galileans were despised in Jerusalem as provincial. Most Galileans had a very limited education. But Matthew could read, write, keep records, draw conclusions, weigh the pros and cons of a situation, and make firm decisions. He was used to assessing the value of all the different kinds of merchandise carried by the caravans on the great Damascus-Tyre highway that ran through Capernaum. His work as a tax collector had called for considerable knowledge and he would be an invaluable man to have in the apostolic circle.

Like all other Jews, the disciples had well-trained and retentive memories and would be able to recall much of what they heard and saw in their three and a half years with Jesus—especially when their capacious memories were quickened by the Holy Spirit. Yet it was in the interest of everyone to have someone along who could write things down. Making notes seems to have been Matthew's particular job, for he never opens his mouth in the Gospels. We see his name in the various lists of the apostles, but we read little else about him.

No sooner had Matthew responded to the royal invitation to become a personal follower of the Christ of God than he did a very sensible thing. He threw a party. He invited all his former friends, the whole fellowship of publicans and sinners, to be his guests. He also invited Jesus and all his new friends in Christ. It was Matthew's way of introducing his former associates to Jesus. It was his way of saying to his old crowd, "I'm through with the old way of life. Come and meet the Master. Come and meet the man who changed my life completely. Perhaps you would like to enthrone Him as Savior and Lord of your lives too."

We have no idea how many responded. Perhaps it was news of Matthew's changed life that touched the heart of Zaccheus. In any case, Matthew's dinner party marked a complete break with his old way of life. He had a new Master, a new fellowship, and new friends. His old friends could come and join him, but he would not be joining them anymore. What a wonderful way to begin a new life in Christ!

Committed now beyond recall, Matthew spent the next three years of his life in the personal company of Jesus and His disciples. He trudged the length and breadth of the promised land with Him. He saw His many miracles (only a scant three dozen of them are recorded in the Gospels). He heard His wonderful sayings. He saw how Jesus handled Himself in various situations. He listened to the sermon on the mount and made copious notes—Matthew was the only Gospel writer to give us the full text. He listened avidly to the Olivet discourse—and again Matthew gave us the fullest account of that remarkable sermon on things to come. He watched the growing opposition. He was in the upper room for the Lord's farewell messages. He had firsthand knowledge of the trial, the terrible miscarriage of justice, the crucifixion, the burial, and the resurrection. And all this time his pen was busy writing and recording. Of the 1,068 verses that make up Matthew's Gospel, 644 contain actual words of Christ, so about three-fifths of his Gospel is made up of the recorded words of the Lord Jesus.

III. HIS MANUSCRIPT

If Matthew never did anything else, he performed a service of the highest order for the world and for the church when he wrote the Gospel that bears his name. His Gospel was initially intended for the Jewish people. He wanted to demonstrate that the man Jesus, whom the Jews had so terribly rejected, was indeed their Messiah. There is ample evidence of this intent in the nature and content of the Gospel itself. Consider the following examples:

1. The Gospel of Matthew traces the Lord's ancestry back to David, the founder of the Hebrew royal family.
2. This Gospel traces that ancestry through Joseph, the lineal descendant of Solomon and the foster father of Jesus.
3. This Gospel makes constant reference to "the holy city" and refers also to "the holy place."
4. This Gospel calls Jesus the Son of David in various places.
5. This Gospel shows the fulfillment of Old Testament prophecy regarding the coming of Christ.
6. This Gospel alone makes reference to the kingdom of Heaven. The kingdom of Heaven is not the same as the kingdom of God. The kingdom of God is eternal, spiritual, and free from sin. It can only be entered by means of the

new birth and its empire is established in the hearts of the regenerate. The phrase "the kingdom of Heaven" refers to God's purpose and plan to establish a kingdom on earth. Its fortunes have fluctuated with the course of history and its establishment is postponed now until the second coming of Christ. Matthew's understanding of the Jewish role in the kingdom of Heaven led him to tell us most of what we know about it.

7. The Gospel of Matthew alludes frequently to Jewish customs, the Mosaic law, and the Hebrew prophets. Matthew generally assumed his readers were familiar with his quotations and allusions.

In all likelihood Matthew's Gospel was written just before the destruction of Jerusalem and the temple by the Romans in A.D. 70. By that time Jewish rejection of the claims of Christ, both in the homeland and among the diaspora, was deeply entrenched.

Matthew's plan was to group his material not necessarily in chronological order, but in a logical order to produce a cumulative effect. For instance, Matthew kept the remarkable sermon on the mount intact, whereas in Luke the substance of the discourse is found scattered here and there throughout the Gospel. Matthew recorded twenty specific miracles of Jesus and, in keeping with his pattern of grouping his material, half of these miracles are recorded in just two chapters (8–9).

Matthew recorded about forty of the Lord's parables. He alone told us about the wheat and the tares, the hidden treasure, the pearl of great price, the fish net, the householder and his treasure, the unmerciful servant, the laborers in the vineyard, the ten virgins, and the talents. Nearly all the parables recorded by Matthew alone are in keeping with his purpose of emphasizing the fact that Jesus was Israel's Messiah.

At least seven of the forty parables recorded by Matthew are parables of judgment. Doubtless the terrors inflicted on his native land as the Romans pursued their relentless war colored

Matthew's writing. Jesus had warned that judgment would come to the apostate nation of Israel. But the judgment at the hand of the Romans was only preliminary. Matthew focused on end-time judgments too. In keeping with the judgmental aspect of his Gospel, Matthew recorded the Lord's denunciations of the Jewish leaders. In this Gospel the Lord's public ministry thus begins with eight beatitudes (Matthew 5:3-10) and climaxes with eight curses (Matthew 23).

Matthew's Gospel can be divided into four parts: (A) in chapters 1–9 the King is revealed; (B) in chapters 10–16 the King is resisted; (C) in chapters 16–27 the King is rejected; (D) in chapter 28 the King is raised.

A. The King Is Revealed

1. His Person

First the Gospel of Matthew reveals _His ancestry_. Jesus was the Son of David and the rightful heir to David's throne. When Matthew wrote, the temple was still standing and anyone could verify the Lord's genealogy by consulting the registers in the temple.

Next the Gospel reveals _His advent_. Matthew recorded how it came to pass that Jesus was born, as prophesied, in the town of Bethlehem. Matthew told of the visit of the wise men from the East—the Gentile magi who bore tribute to Jesus as the King of the Jews. Matthew told also of the fulfillment of another prophecy: "Out of Egypt have I called my son" (Matthew 2:15).

The Gospel then reveals _His ambassador_. Matthew told of the coming of John the Baptist, in the spirit and power of Elijah, to herald the imminent unveiling of the King.

Moreover the Gospel reveals _His adversary_. Matthew gave us the fullest account of how the Lord was tempted in the wilderness and how He routed the ancient enemy of mankind.

2. His Purpose

The King's purpose is revealed in the choice of *His men*. Matthew told us how the Lord chose His disciples, the men with whom He intended to share the administration of His kingdom. Those who judged only by outward appearance thought the disciples were an unpretentious and insignificant collection of nobodies. It was obvious that here was a King who loved ordinary folk. He bypassed the religious establishment as represented by synagogue and Sanhedrin and went straight to the common people for His followers.

Matthew also revealed *His mandate*. The Gospel records the famous sermon on the mount, in which the King issued a series of astonishing precepts for the government of His kingdom. The Lord took the light of the Mosaic law (in itself impossible to obey completely), passed it through the prism of His divine intellect, broke that white light up into its glowing colors, and then lifted it like a rainbow as high as the heavens themselves. Then in answer to those who wrote the word *impossible* over His precepts, He lived by them— moment by moment, day after day, in all the various circumstances of life.

3. His Power

Then too Matthew revealed the King's power. The Gospel tells how Jesus cleansed the leper, stilled the storm, and raised the dead. He fed the multitudes, healed the sick, and gave sight to the blind. He made the dumb to speak, the deaf to hear, and the lame to walk. Such power had never been demonstrated on earth before.

B. The King Is Resisted

In chapters 10–16 of his Gospel, Matthew wrote of mounting resistance to the King. We would have expected His contemporaries to cheer Him all the way to Jerusalem, Rome, and the empire of the world. Instead the Jewish religious establishment instigated a rising tide of opposition. That resistance was *foretold* in Matthew 10, *felt* in Matthew 11, and *focused* in Matthew 12–13. When the Jewish leaders finally accused Him of doing His marvelous miracles in the power of Satan, He gave a series of parables ("the mystery parables") in which He officially postponed the establishment of the kingdom of Heaven until an unspecified future date. He interposed the age of grace (the church age in which we live), a period of time during which God would work out quite a different purpose of grace—He would build a spiritual *church* rather than establish a material *kingdom*.

C. The King Is Rejected

Matthew 16–27 tells of the King's rejection. After Peter's confession and the subsequent transfiguration, the Lord began to talk increasingly about His forthcoming death on the cross. He pronounced a series of woes upon the leaders of the Jewish religious establishment, and then in His great Olivet discourse He foretold the impending destruction of both Jerusalem and the temple and set the stage for His coming again.

Events happened swiftly after these warnings. Judas defected to the Sanhedrin and betrayed the Lord while He was praying in Gethsemane. A series of mock trials followed and Jesus was handed over by the Romans to the executioners. And so the Jews rejected their Messiah, and the Romans collaborated with them in His murder. An age had come to an end.

D. The King Is Raised

In the final chapter of his Gospel, Matthew told us of the King's resurrection. Matthew 28:1 says it was "the end of the sabbath" when Jesus rose from the dead. It was the end of the sabbath indeed! It was a new dawn, a new day, a new dispensation. Everything now centers not on the dead Jewish sabbath, but on the first day of the week, the resurrection morn, the day the King came back. The Sanhedrin did their best to squelch the tidings, but they might as well have tried to put out the sun. Today the tidings of a risen Christ are heralded around the globe.

Well, Matthew, you took good notes and the Holy Spirit inspired you as to how to use them. We are grateful to you. Little did you know that day when you walked out of the Capernaum customs office that you would eventually write a bestseller—a book that would become part of the divine library, a book that would be read and studied and loved and taught throughout the whole wide world, a book that would be translated into hundreds of languages, a book that would make your name famous for the rest of time. That was a good bargain you made when you forsook all to follow the Christ of God.

---

1. See note 1 on page 38.

6
Jude
the Obscure

Matthew 10:3; Mark 3:18; Luke 6:16; Acts 1:13; John 14:22

I. HIS NAME

II. HIS FAME

    A. A Very Important Test

    B. A Very Important Truth

    C. A Very Important Trio

III. HIS AIM

We can be quite sure that the Lord made no mistakes when He chose the twelve. Indeed He waited some time before He selected His disciples out of an ever-growing crowd of followers and ordained those twelve to be apostles. He made His selections after a night of prayer. Besides, He was incarnate omniscient wisdom. But why did He choose such a pale-faced nonentity as Judas (Jude), the brother (or perhaps son) of James?

Two other men by the name of Judas are prominent in the New Testament: Judas the betrayer, the man who sold the Savior for a handful of coins; and Judas the author of the book of Jude, the little memo on apostasy near the end of the New

Testament. The latter is commonly thought to be one of the Lord's half brothers.

But who was Judas, the son of James? He is barely mentioned outside the lists of the apostles and he is often overlooked by the average reader because in some of the lists he is not called Judas.

I. HIS NAME

He bore a name of infamy. After the nefarious and notorious behavior of Judas Iscariot, the name Judas was a heavy enough cross for anyone to carry. "Oh! So you're Judas?" people might say, having only heard of the other Judas and not knowing that he was dead.

"No! No!" Jude the Obscure would say. "I'm not *that* Judas."

"Who are you then?"

"I'm Judas the son of James."

The title "Judas the son (or perhaps brother) of James" opens up a complex field of investigation. Three people by the name of James appear in the New Testament. Two of them were disciples of the Lord and one was James the brother of Jesus. This third James was an ascetic. He became prominent in the Jerusalem church and wrote the Epistle that bears his name. He was not one of the Lord's disciples during the days of His earthly ministry and was an unbeliever until the Lord met him and saved him after the resurrection. This James is not thought to have been the father of Judas.

The disciple James the Less was the son of Alphaeus and is sometimes called James the Younger. We know next to nothing about him. Some scholars think that he and Judas were brothers—these relationships are not always so clear as we could wish![1]

Other scholars think that the disciple James who was the brother of John and the son of Zebedee, was the father of Judas. This James, the first martyr among the apostles, was one of the

Lord's inner circle along with Peter and John. If Judas was the son of this James, he was the grandson of Zebedee and the nephew of the apostle John.

If he is undistinguished in all else, this son (or brother) of James is outstanding among the apostles in that he has three names. In Matthew 10:3 he is called "Lebbaeus, whose surname was Thaddaeus." In Mark 3:18 he is called Thaddaeus. Luke 6:16 and Acts 1:13 refer to him as "Judas the brother [or son] of James." John 14:22 speaks of "Judas ... not Iscariot." We gather that Judas (Jude), Lebbaeus, and Thaddaeus are all names for the same individual, for the names always appear in the same position in the various listings of the twelve.

Perhaps out of kindness and consideration Matthew and Mark dropped the name Judas. Luke used it to help us identify the man. John wrote at the end of the first century when it no longer mattered that there were two men by the name of Judas, one of whom was infamous and the other more or less anonymous. By that time Jude the Obscure may have been dead. Just the same, out of respect for the memory of the faithful Judas, John distinguished him from the traitor by adding the words "not Iscariot."

Both *Thaddaeus* and *Lebbaeus* suggest the idea of being dear or beloved or close to the heart. Probably these were nicknames given to Judas either when he was young or after he became an apostle. In any case he apparently was looked upon with affection.

Jesus deliberately chose this Judas. If he was the grandson of Zebedee and Salome, Jesus knew him well. Salome was His mother's sister. So Jude's grandmother was the Lord's aunt, his grandfather was the Lord's uncle, and Jude's father James was the Lord's cousin! During the silent years of Jesus' life, He and His family must have made many trips from Nazareth to the seaside to visit His mother's family. Jesus would often have observed little Judas growing up. Perhaps He saw in him the character traits that earned the nickname Thaddaeus. Judas may well have been a lovable little fellow. Jesus and young

Judas were attracted to each other, and by the time Jesus was ready to call James to be a disciple, He had made up His mind to call young Judas as well.

Jesus knew Judas would never be a boisterous leader like Peter. He would never be a great visionary like his uncle John. He would never stand tall or stand out, but Jesus saw something in him. When we get to the judgment seat of Christ and the books are opened, we will understand why Jesus added this youngster to the apostolic band. Perhaps Jesus valued his youthfulness, which made him quiet and retiring around the older men. Perhaps Jesus desired diversity in age as well as in temperament and background among the twelve. In any case Judas found his place among the disciples. He was a follower rather than a leader, a listener rather than a talker. Indeed he only spoke once in Scripture, but what he said was very much to the point, as we will see.

Judas Iscariot tarnished a great name: that of Judah. Young Jude the Obscure went a long way to redeem it. *Judas, Judah,* and *Jude* are synonymous. Judah was the name of the royal tribe, the tribe of which Jesus was born.

II. HIS FAME

Judas is famous for only one thing: a question. Only once in the Gospels did he speak, and then it was to ask Jesus a question. The place was the upper room. The time was the last Passover and the institution of the Lord's supper.

By the following night Jesus would be dead and buried. Within an hour He would be weeping His heart out in Gethsemane. Soon Peter, usually so forward, would have denied the Lord three times, once with oaths and curses. Only Jude's uncle John would show any semblance of courage and he would become the tender guardian of Mary, the Lord's mother. Judas Iscariot would be both dead and damned—his name blotted out of God's book and indelibly written into the history of this world as the archetype of all traitors. In time and one by one the scattered disciples would find their way back to this upper room. Jude the Obscure and the other disciples—wishing they were as obscure as he was—would huddle there behind barred and bolted doors dreading to hear the footfall of the temple police or of Pilate's officers.

But let us refocus on Jesus sharing the last Passover meal with His disciples. Once Judas Iscariot had left their midst, a sense of foreboding prevailed in the upper room. Jesus addressed a hushed and unhappy group. "I'm going away," He said in effect. "I'm going home. But don't let that bother you too much. You know both where My Home is and how to get there." He went on to speak of other things. He told them about the Holy Spirit. He told them they could expect the hatred of the world. He talked to them about the true vine. He prayed for them. Jude the Obscure sat there at the table with all the others listening, hardly believing his ears, wondering what kind of world it would be without Jesus.

The Lord was interrupted three times. First Thomas *contradicted* Him. He told the Lord He did not know where He was going and certainly didn't know the way. Then Philip *confronted* Him. He said in effect: "You keep on talking about the Father. Who is this Father You talk about? Show Him to us and we'll be satisfied." Then Jude *consulted* Him. He asked Him a question.

There are various kinds of questions. The *scientist* asks why. Why does a magnetized needle point north? Why does light travel at the speed of 186,000 miles per second? Why does the gravity of the earth attract a falling object?

The *pragmatist* asks how. "So what if the square on the hypotenuse is equal to the sum of the squares of the two sides containing the right angle!" he says. "How does that fact affect practical everyday life?" The answer to his question leads him to the three-four-five-triangle, which enables him to lay out perfectly angled ninety-degree buildings.

The scientist asks why mass and energy and the speed of light are interrelated, and he comes up with an equation that explains the relationship of space, matter, and time. The pragmatist says how that equation relates to the real workaday world, and he invents the atomic bomb and the nuclear power plant.

Jude the Obscure heard what Jesus was saying. He followed the conversation and the interruptions. He heard Jesus say, "He that hath my commandments, and keepeth them, he it is that loveth me: and he that loveth me shall be loved of my Father, and I will love him, and will manifest myself to him" (John 14:21). The word "manifest" arrested young Judas. The original Greek word *emphanizō* means "to cause to be manifest or shown plainly and clearly; to see something that otherwise would not be recognized by the unaided mind or eye." Jude quickly extrapolated something of profound significance: Those who loved the Lord and were loved by Him would be enabled to see things hidden from the general run of men and women. This revelation of the Lord Jesus, in other words, would be a secret revelation.

At once Judas asked his question: not why, but how. "Lord, how is it that thou wilt manifest thyself unto us, and not unto the world?" (John 14:22) The question was penetrating and went to the heart of the matter.

All the disciples had expected the Lord to manifest Himself to the world. They had anticipated an earthly kingdom. They had looked forward to the day when He would come suddenly into the temple, announce Himself as the promised Messiah, take over the reigns of government from the ruling and unbelieving establishment, mobilize His forces, rid the country of the Romans, sit on the throne of His father David, and extend His empire to the ends of the earth. Doubtless Judas had gulped at the revelation that Jesus intended to do no such thing now. He could take in his youthful stride the total upset of all the conventional ideas about the Messiah. But the practical problem remained: How could Jesus possibly manifest Himself to some people and not to other people? And how could He show Himself if He was going home to Heaven?

The Lord did not deal with Jude's question directly. The answer on the pragmatic earthly level would be known soon enough. Within the next few days and weeks, the resurrection, the ascension, and the coming of the Holy Spirit would answer Jude's question more fully than anything the Lord could say that night. Moreover Jude and the others would be better equipped to understand the answer later on.

The last time the world saw Christ was when the authorities sealed Him into Joseph's tomb and set a guard to patrol the grounds. Nobody witnessed Christ's resurrection. Early in the morning just as the dawn was tinting the eastern sky, Jesus rose through the graveclothes and stepped silently and invisibly through the walls of the tomb. Nobody saw Him rise. For some time afterward the sentries continued to patrol up and down before an empty tomb. They did not know it was empty until the angel came and rolled back the stone to show to one and all that the tomb was tenanted no more. One sight of that angel was enough for even those Roman veterans. With a howl of terror they fled toward the city.

Then Jesus began to manifest Himself to His followers. He manifested Himself in His *resurrection* body. He appeared here and there to this one and to that one. He appeared to Peter and to James. He appeared to the two on the Emmaus road. He appeared in the upper room. He appeared again to convince Thomas. He appeared by the shore of the sea of Galilee. On one occasion He manifested Himself to about five hundred believers at one time, but never to the world.

He also manifested Himself in His *rapture.* He gathered the entire band of believers together and led them to the mount of Olives. He talked and answered questions as He went. Then right before their eyes He stepped from the earth into the sky and thence back into Heaven.

The Lord manifested Himself in *revelation* as well. In the upper room on the day of Pentecost the Holy Spirit came. The eyes of the disciples' understanding were then fully opened. They understood at last and in the full blaze of that understanding went out to evangelize the world and write the various books of the New Testament.

Jude the Obscure, of course, was to be in on all these events. The Lord had no need to give an explanation ahead of time. Everything would be made plain in the course of the next six or seven weeks. Instead the Lord went to the heart of Jude's question and taught him some very important lessons that are recorded in John 14:23.

A. A Very Important Test

"If a man love me," He said, "he will keep my words." This statement presents the ultimate test of genuine love for the Lord: Those who love the Lord do what He says. Those who love the Lord treasure His Word. His slightest wish is their command. Love can never do enough for the Beloved. If we say we love Him but spend little time reading His Word and even less time doing what He says, there is something radically wrong with what we call love.

B. A Very Important Truth

"If a man love me, he will keep my words," Jesus said, "and my Father will love him." Imagine being the special object of the love of the Father. The Lord Jesus was always talking about His Father. God is rarely called Father in the Old Testament—probably fewer than six times—but the name Father was constantly on the lips of the Lord Jesus. In His first recorded utterance He said to Joseph and Mary, "Wist ye not that I must be about my Father's business?" (Luke 2:49) As a boy of twelve He already knew who His Father was and He had already made it His goal to "do always those things that please him" (John 8:29).

Speaking His last words on the cross He said, "Father, into thy hands I commend my spirit" (Luke 23:46). Jesus spoke the name again in His first conversation after the resurrection. He said to Mary Magdalene, "I am not yet ascended to my Father" (John 20:17). Almost the last word He uttered on earth was

Father. On the way to Olivet He told the disciples to go back to Jerusalem and wait for the promise of the Father. Jesus knew that all times and seasons are in the Father's sphere of authority.

The Lord Jesus loved His Father and His Father loved Him. Now if we love the Lord Jesus with the kind of love that does what He says, and if we treasure His Word, the Father will love us too. He will love us with the *agape* kind of love—the kind of love that is stronger than death, the kind of love that many waters cannot quench, the kind of love that suffers long and is kind. What a truth! Imagine being the object of God's personal affection and tender loving care.

C. A Very Important Trio

"My Father will love him, and we will come unto him, and make our abode with him." What a trio! The Father, the Lord Jesus, and the person who loves the Lord Jesus and does what He says will dwell together. The Father and the Son will come and take up their abode with such a believer.

Think for a moment of what that promise means. God the Father and God the Son will move in with us. They will live in our houses. They will ride in our cars. They will join us where we work. They will be with us when we gather with others of like precious faith. Imagine it! Sometimes we read this awesome statement and hardly let its significance penetrate our minds. The two most wonderful, most powerful, most loving, most infallible persons in the universe will take up their abode with us.[2] They control all the factors of space, matter, and time. They are the objects of the ceaseless adoration of the angels and the theme of the seraphs' song, and they choose to come and live with us!

The word translated "abode" in John 14:23 is the same word that is translated "mansions" in John 14:2. The Father and the Son will turn even the humblest cottage into a mansion, into a place more important by far than the White House or Buckingham Palace.

Jude the Obscure listened to Jesus' words and took them

all in. He said to himself, "I love Him. I intend to do what He says. I love His words. So I'm going to count on having some very exclusive and magnificent company from now on."

III. HIS AIM

Aided after Pentecost by the baptizing, indwelling, filling, and anointing of the Holy Spirit, Judas set out to live the life of one who keeps the words of Christ.

For some time he tarried in Jerusalem with the other apostles. He witnessed the great influx of souls after Pentecost and helped organize and supervise the church. He probably came in contact with Paul and heard his impassioned defense of liberty in Christ for an ever-growing Gentile church. Perhaps Judas and Barnabas had some long talks about the work in Syria, especially in Antioch.

Then the time came to move out of Jerusalem. Reasonably reliable Christian tradition leads us to believe that Jude the Obscure headed north to Syria. He is thought to have helped plant the gospel in Armenia and to have gone to Mesopotamia and Persia. So as Paul headed west with the gospel, this little-known foot soldier of the cross went East. In the end, it is believed, Judas suffered martyrdom in Persia. Wherever he went, this unsung saint of God carried another presence with him. God the Father and God the Son accompanied him on his travels and stood by him in his efforts to spread the glad tidings of salvation.

For the most part Judas remains obscure, but one day the books will be opened. When they are, we will join hands with him around the throne in Heaven and he'll invite us to come along and see his heavenly mansion eternally graced by the abiding presence of the Father and the Son.

---

1. See note 1 on page 38.
2. The coequal Holy Spirit's ministry is not in view in this passage.

7
Simon
the Zealot

Luke 6:15

I. THE MAN HE WAS
II. THE MAN HE MET
III. THE MAN HE BECAME

Simon is called the Zealot and that's all we know about him beyond the fact that he was a disciple of the Lord Jesus and one of the twelve apostles of the Lamb. The silence about him in Scripture is all the more arresting because the other Simon in the apostolic company is made highly visible. The name *Simon* means "one who hears." His name may be some kind of clue to the mystery of the Zealot, for "faith cometh by hearing, and hearing by the word of God" (Romans 10:17). Perhaps we can deduce that he was a good listener, but Scripture does not give us any additional insights. In an attempt to synthesize a character sketch of Simon, we will consider the man he was, the man he met, and the man he became.

As we think of the man Simon was, we will be drawn into *a study of a man's convictions.* We will also see how Jesus CHOOSES a man.

As we think of the man Simon met, we will be undertaking

71

a study of a man's confrontation. We will also see how Jesus
CHALLENGES a man.

As we think of the man Simon became, we will be
engaged in *a study of a man's conversion.* We will also see how
Jesus CHANGES a man.

I. THE MAN HE WAS

When Pompey conquered Judea and Jerusalem, the
country became a Roman province and thereafter its people
were subject to Roman taxation. The Romans paid no attention
to the fact that the Hebrew people were already heavily
taxed— they had to pay a double tithe to support the Levites,
priests, and temple. Most pious Jews paid these religious taxes
willingly enough, but the new tax was harsh and rapacious and
the Romans farmed out the job of collecting it to self-seeking
opportunists. One estimate is that the Jews were paying at least
30 to 40 percent of their income in taxes. So heavy was the
burden that it threatened to bring the country to the verge of
economic collapse. Neither the religious leaders nor the
Roman masters would give way. This is the situation which
gave rise to the Zealots.

The Roman administrators of the country were often
insensitive and heavy-handed. Most of them were hack ap-
pointees—rough-and-ready soldiers who had risen up through
the ranks. They had little or no administrative skill and cared
nothing about social niceties. They made crude mistakes and
backed them up with cruelty. Their idea of statesmanship was
simple: when all else fails, use force.

The Roman procurators were often incompetent. The last
of them, Florus, turned out to be the worst. He had learned
nothing from the history of the previous governors of Judea.
During a Passover celebration he seized the high priest's
vestments. Then Florus added insult to injury by violating with
obscenities the most sacred beliefs of the Jews. He had a
consuming passion for wealth so it is not surprising that he

raided the temple treasury. A riotous demonstration ensued
and Florus chose to treat this demonstration as an act of
rebellion. He called in the troops, arrested a number of the
leading citizens, crucified them, and then handed Jerusalem
over to his soldiers to plunder. This was the last straw and a
revolt against Rome broke out.

The Jews stormed the Roman garrison outside Jerusalem
and routed the troops stationed there. Rebellion spread like fire
throughout the country and the Zealots saw the magic moment
they had been waiting for. They captured the impregnable
fortress of Masada. The tiny Jewish nation had thrown down
the gauntlet to Rome, the giant oppressor of the world, and the
Zealots became national heroes.

This group of rebels was the party Simon had joined. The
Zealots were an intolerant crowd. Josephus described them as
sicarii, a term that refers to people armed with daggers. Until
open insurrection against Rome was possible, the more extreme Zealots relied on simple terrorism to achieve their ends.
These extremists would conceal daggers in their robes, mingle
with the crowds, and stab those they regarded as traitors.

The Zealots were in the thick of the fight against Rome.
At the time the Roman army drew its compass around
Jerusalem, the city was in the hands of three rival groups: the
city itself was in the hands of Simon Bar Giora; the outer temple
court was held by John of Gischala; and the inner courts were
held by the Zealot leader Eliezer ben Simon. The unfortunate
people of Jerusalem suffered as much from the brigandry,
oppressions, and squabbles of these bandit leaders as they did
from the Roman siege. When the three rival gangs were not
fighting Rome, they were fighting each other and pillaging and
ravaging the inhabitants of the city. Anyone suspected of
wanting to defect to Rome was killed—often simply flung over
the wall of the city to be dashed to pieces by the rocks below.
The scenes of horror and terror inside the city were almost
indescribable. Josephus heaped much of the blame for the
suffering on the Zealots.

The last stand of the Zealots was at Masada in A.D. 71. After a long and bitter fight the fortress was taken by the Roman general Silva. Masada, a remote "fortress in the sky" in one of the most desolate places on earth, frowned down on the Dead Sea. Herod the Great had made the fortress virtually impregnable and the Romans were compelled at last to build an enormous and expensive ramp up to the walls. When they finally stormed the fortress, they found only a few people still alive. All the rest had committed suicide rather than fall into the hands of the Romans. To this day the Zealots' defense of Masada is legendary.

Simon was a Zealot, but not all Zealots were nationalist fanatics. Some were pure idealists. However all of them longed to see their country forever rid of the Romans.

When Jesus decided to pour Himself into just a dozen men, one of the men He chose was Simon the Zealot. Simon, after all, was a man of conviction. He may have been inclined to carry his convictions to the extreme, but the beliefs he held, he held with passion. Jesus needed a man like him.

On the purely human level Simon might have been a potential liability to Jesus. We can be sure that the procurator's palace had a list of men to be kept under surveillance and high on this list were members of the Zealot party. They were known troublemakers, forever fomenting riot and rebellion. To be marked down as a Zealot in those days would be like being marked down as a Jew by the Nazis or as a communist in the days of the cold war. Jesus took the risk in His stride. He was as willing to associate Himself with a Zealot as with a publican.

There was considerable variety within the ranks of the apostolate. Simon was a Zealot; Matthew was a publican. They stood at opposite ends of the political spectrum. One was an ardent patriot, the other an outcast collaborator. Peter was a doer; John was a dreamer. Nathanael was a thinker. Thomas was a doubter. Philip was a realist, Andrew was an optimist, and Judas Iscariot was an opportunist. They were as diverse a collection of men as you would find today in the average local church.

Yet they all were attracted to Jesus, and Jesus was attracted to them. He chose them after a night of prayer. He knew what He was doing when He called Simon the Zealot. He knew the man's secret heart. He knew that he ached and longed for the Messianic kingdom. He knew that the spark and fire that made him a Zealot would also make him a grand apostle—once all his fiery passions had been extinguished and rekindled by Calvary love.

Simon the Zealot was made out of the same stuff as the Old Testament prophet Jonah, a man who was fearless, single-minded, and mightily used of God. Jesus had a future field of service for a man like him.

So we can surmise what kind of man Simon was: a man of conviction. We never read anything about him except that Jesus chose him and called him—and he came. We do not know how long Jesus knew him or when he was called. We do not know what kind of home he came from. We do not know if he moved in the same circles as Barabbas and his band of insurrectionists. We do not know anything except that he was willing to lay all his passionate convictions at Jesus' feet. In the Gospels he never raised his voice in debate. He never pushed himself forward. He asked no questions. Simon ("one who hears") was just there—listening, learning, longing, looking.

II. THE MAN HE MET

Before Jesus began His public ministry, a notable prophet appeared among the Jews—his voice raised in the wilderness, his message strangely stirring to the soul, and his appeal widespread among the masses. "Repent," John the Baptist cried, "for the kingdom of heaven is at hand" (Matthew 3:2). Thousands of people were moved to the depths of their beings. They flocked in droves to the Jordan to hear him. Large numbers responded to his call for baptism as a token of repentance.

The fact that the religious establishment wrote John off as a public nuisance probably helped confirm to Simon the Zealot that the man was indeed a true prophet of God in the Old Testament sense of the word. The Sanhedrin and the synagogue had sunk to a sorry level of compromise, materialism, hypocrisy, formalism, and impotence, so Simon would be inclined to listen to John. Perhaps Simon thought that John was the prophet Elijah who was to herald the coming of the Messiah. Probably Simon determined to keep his eyes and ears open.

Then Jesus came. He took up John's cry: "The kingdom of heaven is at hand." John did no miracles and he kept himself in the backwoods and in the wilderness. But the new teacher, Jesus of Nazareth, took the Jewish world by storm. Stories of miracles came pouring in from all over. Not even in the days of Moses and Elijah had such wonders been seen. It seemed that neither demons nor disease nor even death could exist in His presence. Moreover He was preaching about a kingdom now being offered to Israel. The common people heard Him gladly. The establishment suspended judgment, but as usual were inclined to be negative.

Perhaps the action of Jesus in the temple in Jerusalem finally persuaded Simon the Zealot of His authenticity (John 2:14-17). Jesus looked around the courts with growing wrath. He used a scourge of cords to drive out the money-changers and overturned their tables. He drove out the merchants who marketed sacrificial animals. "Make not my Father's house an house of merchandise," He said. When Simon the Zealot heard about the cleansing of the temple, he said to himself, "Good for Him!" Perhaps Simon remembered the Old Testament text about the promised Messiah: "The zeal of thine house hath eaten me up" (Psalm 69:9). Here was a Zealot indeed.

Perhaps the Lord's social program first appealed to Simon. Here was a man who was actually doing something about the sick and the hungry. What had the Zealots ever done? True, they were against injustice, tyranny, and the Roman occupation of their native land. The program of the Zealots, however, seemed to begin and end with clandestine meetings. It was a program of deception, violence, guerilla warfare, and for those who were caught, a cross.

One day the confrontation came. Jesus challenged Simon to become one of His disciples. We know nothing whatever about the meeting. We can be quite sure, however, that Jesus made the issues crystal clear. He was the last, the rightful, and the only surviving legitimate claimant to David's throne—a fact that could be checked by consulting the records in the temple—and He was going to establish a kingdom. He was indeed the Messiah, the King of Israel. He was the Son of God.

Simon was being invited to become part of a revolution! However, unlike any other revolution, this was to be a revolution of love. The problem was much more serious than the Roman occupation. The problem was sin. Jesus had come to destroy sin's empire in the human heart.

Doubtless Jesus said much the same to Simon the Zealot as He said to Nicodemus: "Except a man be born again, he cannot see the kingdom of God" (John 3:3). Jesus was indeed going to found an empire—but the ruling principle in that empire was to be love. There would be a revolution, but it would be based on regeneration. Human nature has to be changed before nations can be changed.

Simon certainly had a lot to think about. He also had to consider that indefinable "something" about Jesus. It was not just His clear thinking, His great vision, His captivating personality, and His demonstrated power. It was not just His radiant humanity. There was His evident deity. He was so essentially good. Indeed *holy* would be a better word to describe Him. His wisdom, love, and power were absolute, beyond any ever displayed by sinners of Adam's ruined race.

So Simon the Zealot made his decision for Christ. Then Jesus must have introduced him to the others. "This is Simon

Peter and his brother Andrew, fishermen from Capernaum. This is James and his brother John. Their mother Salome and My mother are sisters. They too used to be fishermen. This is Thomas. These two are Philip and Nathanael. Here's someone you'll be interested to meet: Matthew or Levi, to give him his Hebrew name. He used to be a tax collector, a publican, but now he is My disciple and My friend. Here's Judas. We have two Judases. This one is Judas Iscariot. He's our treasurer ... "

Under any other circumstances and in any other setting, the Zealot would have had little or nothing in common with most of these men. What made him one of them, and one with them, was their common love for the Lord Jesus. The apostles were like the spokes of a wheel, radiating out from their common center to the circumference of the circle. As those spokes draw closer and closer to the hub, they draw closer and closer to each other. They depict the secret of the apostolic community. Each of the twelve, except Judas Iscariot, loved the Lord Jesus. He was the hub that held them all together. As they drew nearer to Him, they drew nearer to each other. Apart from Him there would have been no apostolate. Apart from Him there can be no church.

Simon the Zealot accepted Christ's challenge. He exchanged his membership in a band of hotheaded revolutionaries for membership in a fellowship based on love for the Lord Jesus Christ. He would never regret his decision. The man he met became all-in-all to him. The man he met eclipsed all others, dominated all horizons, controlled all situations, filled his heart and mind, and thenceforth ruled his life—for the man he met was Jesus!

III. THE MAN HE BECAME

Conversion is both a crisis and a process. The crisis comes when Jesus is enthroned in the heart as Savior and Lord. The process goes on for the rest of the believer's life. The crisis is often sudden; the process is usually slow. We grow in grace and increase in the knowledge of God. Both growing and acquiring knowledge are gradual processes.

Surely it did not take Simon long to realize that his zeal would need to be redirected. The sermon on the mount must have convinced him of his need. It would take the death, burial, resurrection, and ascension of Christ, followed by the baptism, indwelling, filling, and anointing of the Holy Spirit to bring him and the other apostles into some measure of the fullness of the stature of Christ.

Tradition tells us that after the concentration of the apostles in Jerusalem was finally broken up and the apostles began to take seriously the Lord's call to "the uttermost part of the earth" (Acts 1:8), Simon the Zealot headed for North Africa. He journeyed westward through what was called Mauretania and probably took the gospel to the great city of Carthage. Then Simon and Joseph of Arimathaea, it seems, went to Britain.

Britain had been conquered by Julius Caesar half a century before the birth of Christ. London was founded in A.D. 43 and within a couple of decades became an important city. When Nero became emperor the British people, led by the indomitable Queen Boadicea, revolted against Roman rule and a savage war broke out. About this time Simon would have arrived in Britain with the gospel.

One tradition is that the Zealot's activities were brought to the attention of Caius Decius, who nursed in his pagan soul a deep hatred of Christianity. Simon was arrested, given a mock trial, and sentenced to death by crucifixion. He is said to have been martyred at Caistor, Lincolnshire, where he was buried on or about May 10, A.D. 61.

A different tradition is that he did preach to the Latin community in Britain, perhaps even in London, but the Boadicea uprising prompted him to leave the country since the climate was no longer favorable to the gospel. Simon is thought to have returned to Palestine and made his way to Persia, where he was martyred by being sawn asunder.

Simon remained zealous to the end. His vision for the liberation of Palestine from the rule of Rome was expanded by Christ to a vision for the salvation of the whole lost Gentile world. Once he advocated the use of the sword, but after his conversion he proclaimed God's offer of peace to all mankind.

The church needs men like Simon the Zealot. So many Christians are lazy, apathetic, half-hearted, and careless; they cannot find it in their hearts to give even minimal support to the evangelistic and Bible-teaching efforts of the church. We need the zeal of a John Knox, who said, "Give me Scotland or give me death!" We need men like D. L. Moody; when he heard someone say that the world had yet to see what God could do through a man wholly sold out to Him, he declared, "By the grace of God I'll be that man." We need men like David Livingstone, who was willing to go anywhere as long as it was forward. We need men like George Verwer, who motivated thousands to get up and get going for God; he was driven by the life-text, "Nothing shall be impossible unto you" (Matthew 17:20). The church needs men who are willing to be fuel for the flame of God.

8
Thomas
the Twin

John 11:16; 14:1-6; 20:24-29

```
I. HIS CAUTION
II. HIS COMMITMENT
III. HIS CONCERN
IV. HIS COLLAPSE
V. HIS CONFESSION
```

He is usually called Thomas, but sometimes Didymus. Both names mean "the twin." Because he is usually paired with Matthew in the various listings of the twelve apostles in the New Testament, it has been surmised that he was perhaps the twin brother of Matthew.

One commentator, Matthew Poole, speculated that Matthew was the original prodigal son, for before his conversion Matthew was a renegade Jew who had sunk so low as to sell his soul to Rome. The far country is not always defined in terms of miles; it can often be defined in terms of morals. If Matthew was indeed the prototype for the prodigal in the Lord's parable, Thomas (if he was Matthew's twin) must have been the original elder brother. In the case of twins, being the elder brother can hinge on a matter of minutes. Esau and Jacob were twins, but

Esau was always considered the elder and Jacob the younger even though their births were only minutes apart. These are interesting speculations, but probably nothing more.

Archbishop Trench saw a connection in Thomas between being a twin and being twin-minded. The twins of belief and unbelief battled each other in Thomas's heart just as Esau and Jacob struggled in Rebekah's womb. Regardless of whether there is any truth in these suggestions, the fact remains that Thomas was a twin and that somewhere he had a twin brother or twin sister. It would be interesting to know whether he or she also became a follower of the Lord Jesus.

We are indebted to the apostle John for all we know about Thomas as a person. The synoptic writers only mentioned him in their various listings of the twelve apostles. John, writing toward the end of the first century and looking back to those wonderful years of his youth, evidently thought of Thomas as one who was a personality in his own right. Perhaps they had been boyhood friends, since both were Galileans.

I. HIS CAUTION

We call him Doubting Thomas, but it might be fairer to say he was cautious. He always wanted to be sure of his ground. He was not the kind of man to sign a document without first reading it all the way through. In a debate his favorite defense would be "Prove it!" He was the kind of man who had to see things for himself. Once he was convinced, he would hold tenaciously to what he believed.

It is not a bad idea to be cautious, especially about what we accept as the articles of our faith. The Bible urges us to be cautious. In his first Epistle John warned against deceiving spirits that lurk in the unseen world. He warned us not to accept ideas just because they were imparted by ecstatic utterance or by a so-called prophet. The Holy Spirit commended the people of Berea because they put even the preaching of an apostle to the test. They searched the Scriptures daily to see if the teachings of Paul were true.

There was a high brick wall around the playground of the high school I attended in Britain. The wall was topped with a thick layer of cement in which was embedded pieces of jagged broken glass. The idea, of course, was to discourage boys from scaling the wall. I once saw a cat walking along the top. He took each step with great caution. He would put out a paw, gingerly feel the surface, and when he was quite sure that cement and not glass was beneath his feet, he would take the next step. That cat's name might well have been Thomas! Thomas wanted to be sure of his ground before he made a move. There's not much fault to find in that philosophy of life.

But sometimes even the most careful of men will throw all caution to the winds. Thomas did so and thus earned honorable though gloomy commendation in John's memoirs of Jesus.

II. HIS COMMITMENT

It will be helpful to review the circumstances surrounding the time when Thomas made his daring commitment. The Lord Jesus was in Peraea, a rural area beyond the Jordan river. Originally Peraea was the tribal territory of Gad and Reuben. The northern section was densely wooded; the southern section was rich pastureland fading off to widening tracts of desert as the area reached toward the Dead Sea.

Jesus had been up to Jerusalem to keep the feast of tabernacles, a joyful occasion when even Jews from the far-flung lands of the diaspora made their pilgrimage to the holy city to pay their tithes and taxes. The Lord had been watched with great suspicion by the Sanhedrin as He taught in the temple. Their spies were everywhere.

Between the feast of tabernacles and the last Passover feast was a period of about six months, which the Lord spent in Peraea. There His ministry was mostly a teaching ministry devoted to parables and discourses. The time in Peraea was interrupted by a brief visit to Jerusalem in December for the feast of dedication. This feast was personally significant to the Lord Jesus, for it was at the time of His birthday.

There was speculation among the Jews as to whether or not He would come to Jerusalem at all, since official opposition to Him was mounting in the capital. But come He did. He appeared suddenly in the temple and taught the people. He claimed that He was the true Shepherd and they were not His sheep. When He said that He was coequal with the Father, "the Jews took up stones again to stone him" (John 10:31).

He escaped and went back across the Jordan to Peraea. Except for a brief interlude when He went to Bethany to raise Lazarus from the dead, He stayed in Peraea. With the river rolling between Him and His enemies, He gathered the people around Him. There, near the scene of the early labors of John the Baptist and not far from the place where He had been baptized, He taught the people.

What wonderful stories He told on those Peraean hills! We are indebted to Luke for the preservation of most of them. They poured out of Him: stories of the good Samaritan; the importunate neighbor; the rich fool and his barns; the barren fig tree; the great supper and the silly excuses made for not coming; the lost sheep; the lost silver; the lost son; the unjust steward; the rich man and Lazarus; the unjust judge; the self-righteous Pharisee; and the unmerciful servant. Meanwhile the shadows of His rejection were gathering deeper and darker in Jerusalem. The Lord prepared Himself, the people, and His disciples for what lay ahead.

Then came the urgent message: "Lazarus is sick. He's going to die. Please come! Come quickly." But Lazarus was already dead and Jesus knew it. However He sent the messenger back with a word of hope and cheer, and He stayed where He was. The disciples must have breathed a sigh of relief. The last place they wanted to go was the vicinity of

Jerusalem. Two days later Jesus suddenly announced that He intended to go to Bethany to deal with the unfinished business of His friend Lazarus. Immediately a storm of protest arose from the ranks of the disciples. They remembered the angry mob. They could still picture the stones in the hands of the crowd. They could have been stoned with Him.

To his lasting honor, Thomas spoke up. "Let us also go, that we may die with him," he boldly said (John 11:16). Thomas had no doubt whatsoever that if they once ventured back into the vicinity of the capital, the Sanhedrin would orchestrate their death. But if Jesus was determined to go to His death, he was determined to go to his too. Thomas's commitment made him willing to die for Christ if the call of duty demanded such a sacrifice.

So the disciples rallied around this unexpected leader and trooped back toward Jerusalem. Instead of facing the anticipated stoning, they witnessed the greatest of all the Lord's miracles: the resurrection of a man already dead, buried, and decomposing.

III. HIS CONCERN

When Thomas spoke up in Peraea, he spoke with the voice of his heart. When he expressed himself in the upper room, he spoke with the voice of his mind.

So much happened between the two occasions. Jesus entered Jerusalem triumphantly, and the disciples, their hearts pounding with excitement, thought that at last He was going to seize the reins of power and re-establish the throne of David on earth. But the excitement passed and even the densest of them could see that the storm clouds were gathering thick and heavy across their sky. The Sanhedrin was openly plotting to get rid of this unwanted Messiah.

In the upper room Jesus and the disciples observed the Passover and the Lord instituted a new feast of remembrance. The Lord, performing a servant's task to teach a lesson in humility, washed the disciples' feet. Judas departed on his unexplained mission.

Then Jesus began to talk again about the subject they dreaded. Over the past few months He had kept coming back to it. He was going to die, by crucifixion of all things. He was going to be buried, but they were not to worry. He would be back three days later. Then He would go home to His Father. "In my Father's house are many mansions," He told them (John 14:2). Although Heaven is infinitely better than earth, in some ways that other world is very much like this one, He assured them.

Adding to the consternation and confusion of the disciples, Jesus said, "Whither I go ye know, and the way ye know" (John 14:4). That was too much for Thomas. He blurted out what was probably on all their minds. They did not have the faintest idea where He was going or how to get there! "We know not whither thou goest," Thomas said. "How can we know the way?" (14:5) In all this incomprehensible talk, one ominous and terrifying fact was clear: He was going away. Thomas spoke up for them all. They did not want Him to go away.

Thomas's outburst gave the Lord Jesus an opportunity to make one of His greatest statements: "I am the way, the truth, and the life: no man cometh unto the Father, but by me" (John 14:6). In His reply to Thomas He answered the three most important questions of the human heart. Man asks, "How can I be saved?" He replies, "I am the way." Man asks, "How can I be sure?" He replies, "I am the truth." Man asks, "How can I be satisfied?" He replies, "I am the life." So long as the disciples knew Him, they knew the way because He was the way.

For a nominal fee one can go into the Hampton Court maze and find out what it is like to be lost. Hampton Court is the famous palace built by Cardinal Wolsey in the days of England's notorious Henry VIII. Having seen the covetous gleam in the king's eye when that imperious monarch saw the palace, Wolsey deeded it over to the king. The maze on the grounds of the palace consists of narrow lanes bordered by high and impenetrable hedges. All paths seem somehow to lead to the middle. When I was quite young an uncle of mine took me into that maze and, sure enough, we ended up in the center where the authorities had thoughtfully provided a seat where one could sit down and think things over. We wandered in the maze for a considerable time and just when I was getting weary, an attendant came along and offered to show us how to get out. Very soon we were on the outside! The secret to all those perplexing pathways was a man—a man who knew the way.

Likewise Jesus knew the way home. In essence Jesus was saying to Thomas and the others, "Don't worry about the way. I am the way. Just follow Me. If you know Me, you know the way because I am the way!"

IV. HIS COLLAPSE

Thomas was almost as overwhelmed by the arrest, betrayal, trial, crucifixion, and burial of Jesus as Peter was. Thomas played the coward and sought to save his own skin, as all the disciples did. Some of them recovered sooner than others and slowly the sad little group began to reassemble in the upper room. They would at least stay around Jerusalem for a few more days to see what might happen. If they kept a low profile, doubtless the authorities would leave them alone.

The Lord's tomb was sealed and guarded. There was no point in going anywhere near it. A couple of days passed. Then early Sunday morning some of the women decided to take the risk. Perhaps they could find someone to open the tomb for them so they could finish embalming the body. Soon they returned with news: the tomb was empty! The guards were gone. The women had seen some angels who told them that Jesus was alive. Peter and John went to see for themselves, but they only saw an empty tomb and some discarded wrappings.

By evening all the disciples were back in the upper

room—all except Thomas. The Lord appeared to them all—all except Thomas. Around that absence of Thomas, scores of suggestions gather themselves and countless sermons have been preached.

Why did Thomas stay away? Why did he make himself the patron saint of believers who stay away from the meetings of the Lord's people? We can suppose that he made the usual excuses people make today.

Thomas might have said, "I'm too tired, too overwrought. This has been a terrible few weeks. I need a rest." Or "I'm too busy. I have to get my life reorganized and pick up the threads of my old fishing business." Or "It's too dangerous to go out right now. The political and religious climate in Jerusalem is particularly unhealthy for believers in Jesus of Nazareth. The city is swarming with Sanhedrin spies. Why, the moment I step outside this house I'm likely to be arrested. I didn't mind dying for Christ when there was still time for another miracle to happen. But all hope for a miracle is gone." Or "I'll stay home and read my Bible. I can get just as much out of Moses and the Psalms as I would get out of a meeting with the others. All they'll do is pool their ignorance anyway. Besides, Peter will probably be there and he'll do all the talking. The last thing I need is to hear that man talk after the way he cursed and swore the other day. But he'll be up at the front as bold as brass telling everybody what to do." Or "It's going to rain." Or "I can't imagine a meeting without Jesus in the midst. Any meeting without Him will be dead and dull and meaningless."

So Thomas stayed home and missed Jesus. That evening He came in—through the walls! He talked to those who were there, let them handle Him, ate a meal, and vanished. And Thomas missed everything.

We can be sure that when he did bump into one of the other disciples and heard the astounding news, he was quite taken aback. Then his native caution would have come to his aid. He would have said, "I don't believe it. You are all mistaken. You've been seeing things." The united testimony of the other ten made no impression on him at all. "Except I shall see in his hands the print of the nails, and put my finger into the print of the nails, and thrust my hand into his side," he said, "I will not believe" (John 20:25).

The first time Thomas spoke, he spoke with the voice of his heart (John 11:16). The second time he spoke with the voice of his mind (14:5). Now we hear the voice of his will. In the last analysis, the outcome of the battle between doubt and faith always hinges on the will. We doubt, not because we *cannot* believe, but because we *will not* believe.

V. HIS CONFESSION

Thomas did not miss the next meeting. The following Sunday he was in his place in the upper room, as skeptical as ever, but there just the same. He was still muttering to himself, "I won't believe. I have to see. I have to feel...."

Then all of a sudden Jesus was there in the midst of the disciples! The doors were barred and bolted. There was no knock at the door, no hailing voice asking to be let in. He was just there! Having proved His omnipotence by coming through a barred and bolted door, He proved His omniscience by singling Thomas out and responding to his skeptical words: "Reach hither thy finger, and behold my hands; and reach hither thy hand, and thrust it into my side: and be not faithless, but believing" (John 20:27). Sad to say, the Lord used the same word (translated "faithless") He had used to describe the chronic unbelief of the world in Matthew 17:17.

Thomas was won over. "My Lord and my God," he exclaimed (John 20:28), placing Jesus on the throne of his heart ("my Lord") and on the throne of the universe ("my God"). "Thomas," the Lord rejoined, "because thou hast seen me, thou hast believed: blessed are they that have not seen, and yet have believed" (20:29).

We of course are among the blessed. We are in that succession of multitudes of men, women, boys, and girls who have believed without seeing—who have simply taken God's word that the gospel is true. With all such believers the Lord is well-pleased.

After John 20:28 the Bible records no more words spoken by Thomas. It does, however, include his name in John 21:2 and in the roll call of the apostles present in the upper room on the day of Pentecost (Acts 1:13). He was, therefore, one of those upon whom the Holy Ghost came with mighty power.

Eventually, tradition says, Thomas went eastward with the gospel—first to Babylon, then across the Euphrates to Parthia, and then on to India. Everywhere he went he told about the One who was risen from the dead, who could walk through walls, who still wears the nail scars in His hands, and who is now in Heaven preparing a place of many mansions. All Thomas's doubts were replaced by certainties once Jesus became not only his Lord but also his God.

9
John
the Beloved

John 1:35-39

I. JOHN AS A PERSON

II. JOHN AS A PUPIL

III. JOHN AS A PASTOR

    A. A Word about the Fellowship

    B. A Word about the Faith

    C. A Word about the Family

IV. JOHN AS A PROPHET

V. JOHN AS A PRISONER

By the time John took up his pen to write his Gospel, his Epistles, and the Apocalypse, the first century of the Christian era was about to close. As an old man he looked out on a world much different from the one he had known as a boy. Jerusalem was no more. The Jewish people had been uprooted and scattered to the ends of the earth. The church was spreading over the entire world and had already endured the terrible persecutions of Nero and Domitian. The roots of apostasy were everywhere. Gnosticism threatened to change Christianity into something unrecognizable. Peter was gone, James was gone, and the apostle Paul was gone.

John wrote for the third generation of Christians. By its third generation a movement stands in desperate need of revival or else it will either disappear altogether or linger on as a ghost of its former self. In the first generation truth is a *conviction.* Those who hold a conviction, hold it dearly. They do not know the meaning of compromise. They are willing to die for what they believe to be true. In the second generation the conviction becomes a *belief.* Sons hold to the truths they have been taught by their fathers and defend their beliefs in discussion and debate. However the keen edge of conviction has been blunted and adherence to a body of beliefs inherited from the fathers is not so much a passion as a persuasion. In the third generation the belief becomes an *opinion.* By then some members of the movement are willing to trade their opinions in. They feel it is time for a change, they start talking about renewal, and they look to the world for ideas.

John wrote for this third generation. He wrote with a sense of urgency. He did not write, as did the synoptists, from the viewpoint of an infant church; he wrote from the standpoint of an infirm church, one that was in dire peril from persecution without and subversion within.

We will look at John as a person, as a pupil, as a pastor, as a prophet, and as a prisoner.

I. JOHN AS A PERSON

His father was Zebedee, a successful fisherman of Bethsaida on the sea of Galilee. His mother was Salome. She had ambitious plans for her son. A devoted follower of the Lord Jesus, she sometimes traveled with the apostles. She was present at the crucifixion and at the tomb on resurrection morning. From Matthew 27:56, Mark 15:40, and John 19:25 it may be inferred that she was a sister of Mary, the mother of Jesus. John's brother was James, the first of the apostles to pay the price of martyrdom. The two brothers appear to have been cousins of the Lord Jesus, so they doubtless had known Him most of their lives. The Zebedee family was prosperous. They had hired servants and ministered unto the Lord of their substance (Luke 8:3). Moreover they were influential in official circles in Jerusalem.

A follower of John the Baptist before becoming a follower of Jesus, John the Beloved was one of the first two disciples to be called by Christ (John 1:35-39; Matthew 4:18-22). Along with his brother James and Simon Peter, John was one of the inner circle of three in the apostolic fellowship and as such was given a special vision of the Lord's *greatness* at the raising of Jairus's daughter, of the Lord's *glory* on the mount of transfiguration, and of the Lord's *grief* in the garden of Gethsemane.

John was one of the four who prompted the Olivet discourse by asking the Lord questions about eschatology (Mark 13:3). John was one of the two sent by the Lord to prepare for the Passover (Luke 22:8). John was called "the disciple whom Jesus loved" (John 21:20) and he was the disciple to whom the Lord Jesus entrusted the care of His mother (John 19:25-27). Although John was of a contemplative disposition, he was capable of being greatly aroused—so much so that Jesus called him "a son of thunder" (see Mark 3:17).

John was with Peter when Peter healed the lame man at the temple gate (Acts 3:1). John appeared before the Sanhedrin with Peter (Acts 4) and the two refused to obey the command to cease from speaking in the name of Jesus. John went with Peter to Samaria to give the apostolic blessing to the Samaritan revival spearheaded by Philip the evangelist (Acts 8:14).

John was banished to the island of Patmos by the emperor Domitian and died a natural death at Ephesus during the reign of the emperor Trajan (A.D. 98-117).

II. JOHN AS A PUPIL

If we were to ask John what he learned during the three and a half amazing years he spent with Jesus, he would point us to that wonderful book we know as the Gospel of John. In that Gospel we have John's memoirs of Jesus. John wrote his Gospel when he was an old man, but he had forgotten nothing. Indeed he had mused over the miracles of Jesus and meditated deeply on His teachings for many years. A remarkable memory, quickened by the Holy Spirit, enabled John to write a Gospel that was *contemplative, complementary* to the works of Matthew and Mark and Luke, and *conclusive* regarding the gnostic heresy.

John's Gospel is the basis of our chronology of the life of Christ. We gather from this Gospel that the Lord ministered for three and a half years. John recorded the Lord's visits to Jerusalem in connection with the national feasts, and from him we learn that Jesus had six periods of ministry in Judea, five in Galilee, one in Samaria, and one in Peraea.

John's favorite words were *know* (used 142 times), *believe* (used 100 times), *Father* (used 118 times), *world* (used 78 times), *see* (used 105 times), *verily* (used 50 times in 25 pairs), and *love* (used 36 times).

John struck the dominant notes in his Gospel again and again. Pre-eminently he wanted to demonstrate the fact that Jesus was indeed whom He claimed to be: the Son of the living God. The miracles and messages of Jesus in John's Gospel were carefully chosen to this end.

The thoughts, imagery, and language in John's Gospel were drawn from the Old Testament. Graham Scroggie said that there are probably 124 references rooted in the Old Testament. Seven times John referred to Scripture being fulfilled.

Scroggie also pointed out that John evidently had Luke's Gospel in front of him when he wrote his Gospel. What Luke put in, John left out; what Luke left out, John put in.[1]

It is from John that we learn how our Lord Jesus (as man) made Himself available to the Father, so that God could in turn make Himself available to the Son. Now we can enjoy the same type of relationship. As men we can make ourselves available to Jesus so that He (as God) can make Himself available to us.

John taught us nearly all we know about the Father and

much of what we know about the Holy Spirit. John was the one who emphasized the absolute deity of the Lord Jesus.

The Gospel of John revolves around three focal points: the signs, the secrets, and the sorrows of the Son of God. John first set before us various *signs* and proofs that Jesus of Nazareth was the One who was in the beginning with God, who was God, and who became flesh and dwelt among us as God incarnate. Then John set before us the *secrets* revealed in those heart-to-heart upper-room talks of Jesus with His disciples prior to His crucifixion. Finally John set before us the *sorrows* of the Son of God as he bypassed Gethsemane and took us straight to the trials and the tree.

John was a very good pupil! By the time he started to write his Gospel, he had been taught not only by the Son of God but also by the Spirit of God. Because he was a good student he was able to give us facts that the synoptic writers omitted from their narratives and to show us the Lord's thought-life. John's Gospel is of incomparable worth.

John lingered long at the cross. One half of his Gospel is devoted to just one week in the Lord's life: Passion week. To him the great wonder of the universe was that the Son of God should die for sinful man.

III. JOHN AS A PASTOR

In the New Testament a pastor is a shepherd, one who has a heart for the flock. The Lord Jesus is the Chief Shepherd, the great Shepherd of the sheep. A pastor is an undershepherd who cares for the people of God as Jesus cares for them.

When the Lord Jesus from the cross committed the care and keeping of His own mother to His dear friend John, John's work of shepherding began. He took Mary home with him and became a son to her. In later years when John went to Ephesus to help with the pastoral care of the great Pauline church in that city, he may have taken Mary with him. What a blessing that godly woman would have been to that particular flock!

We can formulate an idea of what John was like as a pastor by studying his three Epistles, all of which are short and two of which are little more than memos. His first Epistle deals with fellowship, the second with faith, and the third with family.

A. A Word about the Fellowship

In his first Epistle, as in his Gospel, John took us back to basics. Peter and Paul had both been dead thirty or thirty-five years and John was all alone, the only surviving apostle. Old men dwell much in the past and John referred to the past about fifty times. He referred to "the beginning" ten times (nine of the ten times in connection with Christ and His ministry).

In his Gospel John set forth the life of God *in Christ;* in his first Epistle he set forth the life of God *in us.* The life of God is inherent in Christ; the life of God is imparted to us.

The First Epistle of John gives evidence of its writer's pastoral care. It was written to *banish distance,* for we are called into intimate fellowship with one another and with the Father Himself. It was written to *banish distress* so that the believer's joy might be full. It was written to *banish deception.* One of John's key words is "light" as opposed to darkness. In this Epistle there are no shades of gray. All is black or white, true or false, right or wrong. First John was also written to *banish defilement.* John condemned sin in the life of the believer, called for confession, and reminded us that the blood of Jesus Christ cleanses us from all sin. Finally the Epistle was written to *banish doubt.* John listed about two dozen things we can know. We can know that we have passed from death unto life. We can know that we have been born again.

B. A Word about the Faith

The Second Epistle of John is a brief memo addressed to a lady. Here again we see the pastor at work, for John was concerned about the lady. She was in *danger* since the faith was under attack. It was very likely that she would receive a visit from the emissaries of a cult. Someone would come offering new lamps for old as in the story about Aladdin, so she must be on her guard.

Should such a person come, she should not let him get his foot in the _door_. Christian courtesy did not require her to open the door to a cultist or invite him in to spread forth his wares. The door must be firmly closed on him—in his face if necessary.

When sending this person about his business, she must not even wish him godspeed. She must not shake his hand or bid him good day. The _duty_ of the woman of the house was to send the man packing without even the most common courtesies. John knew how persistent cultists could be. They were not to be given the slightest encouragement to come back.

C. A Word about the Family

The Third Epistle of John is a brief memo addressed to a man. Here again we see in action a great undershepherd of the sheep. We also learn about four men.

The first man is _Gaius the believer_. We are to recognize men like him. Gaius was gentle and hospitable, the kind of man whose ministry is a benediction to a local church.

The second man is _Diotrephes the bully_. We are to resist men like him. He wanted to be a local pope and made it his business to decide who could or could not be received into the fellowship. Diotrephes even prated against the highly esteemed, benevolent, and patriarchal apostle John.

The third man is _Demetrius the brother_. We are to receive men like Demetrius. He seems to have been a traveling preacher whose ministry Diotrephes rejected. John gave Demetrius his own personal word of commendation.

The fourth man is _John the Beloved_. We are to respect men like John. If anyone ever had a right to be a pope it was John, but he held an office better than that of a pope. He was an apostle—and he was not too old to wield the power of an apostle if necessary.

John closed this brief memo with a gentle word. "I hope to see you again before too long," he said in effect. "I plan on coming your way." His glove may have been velvet, but there was a resolute hand in that glove. Many years had passed since John and his brother had been called "the sons of thunder," but let Diotrephes and his kind beware. There are times when even the mildest and most patient of pastors has to assert his authority and power.

John must have been a very good pastor. He had the very best of teachers. He could remember how patiently the Lord had shepherded His own little flock in those far-off Palestinian days. Jesus had even laid down His life for His sheep. John was ready to do the same.

IV. JOHN AS A PROPHET

John was given the task of writing the book that completed the sacred Canon of Scripture. Appropriately enough, Revelation is a book that looks ahead; it is in many ways the greatest book of prophecy in the Bible.

John, as mentioned before, was one of the disciples who asked the question that prompted the Lord to give them His great Olivet discourse. In that sermon on eschatology the Lord Jesus drew together all the threads of New Testament prophecy. Although John never discussed this prophetic discourse in his own Gospel, he doubtless remembered it. Doubtless too he had copies of Matthew's account, and Mark's and Luke's as well.

John's Apocalypse, "the unveiling," is saturated with Old Testament quotations and allusions. The Gospel of Matthew has 92 and the Epistle to the Hebrews has 102, but the Apocalypse has 285 references to the Old Testament. John knew his Bible and must have spent many years poring over its prophecies.

The Apocalypse is closely related to the book of Genesis.

Three chapters from the beginning of Genesis we meet the serpent for the first time. Three chapters from the end of Revelation we meet the serpent for the last time. There are at least two dozen other comparisons and contrasts involving Genesis and Revelation. In Genesis it all begins; in Revelation it all ends.

In the book of Revelation all the forces of Heaven and Hell are seen ranged in conflict and the chief arena of battle is the planet Earth. Arrayed against God's Lamb are the scarlet beast, the scarlet woman, the miracle-working false prophet (with the appearance of a lamb and the voice of a dragon), and the red dragon himself with his seven heads and ten horns! But God's Lamb is no ordinary lamb. This Lamb has seven eyes and seven horns—all the attributes of deity.

Throughout Revelation the scenes alternate between Heaven and earth. God's word is decreed and declared in Heaven and then in spite of all the power of the enemy, His will is done on earth. Revelation unveils the full and final answer to the Lord's prayer: "Thy kingdom come. Thy will be done in earth, as it is in heaven" (Matthew 6:10). But supremely John's prophetic book is an Apocalypse, a Revelation, an unveiling, of Jesus Christ.

The book proceeds in an orderly fashion. First there is a series of seven *seals,* broken so that "the beginnings of sorrows" (Mark 13:8) might overtake the earth. This section of Revelation is all about man. Man reduces the world to a state of utter chaos and the terrified people left on the planet desperately look for any man who can bring order out of chaos.

Then there is a series of seven *trumpets,* blown so that Satan's false messiah, the antichrist, might come and take over the planet. This section of Revelation is all about Satan. He brings his man to total mastery over the globe, inaugurates the great tribulation, and unleashes untold woes on a Christ-rejecting world.

Finally there is a series of seven *vials,* outpoured to bring events to a climax at the final return of Christ. This section of

Revelation is all about God. He steps down at last into the arena of human affairs. He begins to break the antichrist's stranglehold on the planet, mobilizes the Asiatic hordes against him, and draws the armies of the world to Megiddo. When He has His foes where He wants them, He suddenly reappears and puts an end to man's mismanagement of the planet.

The account of John's soaring visions ends with a description of the eternal state and the eternal city—as seen from Heaven's point of view. Thanks to the keen vision of John the prophet, the Bible ends on a triumphant note. The Lord, Revelation tells us, is now sitting on His Father's throne in glory, waiting until the earth is made His footstool.

V. JOHN AS A PRISONER

In the Aegean sea between Asia Minor and Greece, lies a small rocky island called Patmos. About ten miles long and six miles wide, Patmos consists of two segments joined by a narrow isthmus. On this island of rugged volcanic hills and valleys, wrapped by blue waters of the sea, the Romans had a penal colony. Criminals banished to Patmos were compelled to work in its mines and marble quarries. Among the prisoners was the apostle John, who was banished to Patmos by the emperor Domitian in A.D. 95.

We can picture this venerable old man, bowed down beneath his chains, working at hard manual labor all day long. Perhaps out of consideration for his age he was allowed to toil at some lesser task, but we can still picture him as a lonely exile—cut off from his home in Ephesus where he had been respected as a beloved apostle and pastor. Yet this old man was by no means defeated, and we can also picture him out among the angels and the heights of heaven by night.

All the might of Rome could back the emperor's decree banishing the aged apostle to Patmos. But all the power of Hell could not keep John from his dreams and visions. Little did that wicked old tyrant Domitian know that he was setting the stage for a prophet to catch a glimpse of glory!

Tradition says the Romans had tried boiling the apostle in oil, but he had come through unscathed. Over him the tormentor had no power! What could the devil do with a man like John? Turned loose, he would bless the church and win souls to Christ. Martyred, he would be promoted to glory. Locked up in a penal colony, he was "in the isle that is called Patmos" one moment (Revelation 1:9) and "in the Spirit on the Lord's day" the next (1:10). The time will come when we will hear the Lord say, "Well done, John."

---

1. W. Graham Scroggie, *A Guide to the Gospels* (London: Pickering and Inglis, 1948) 426,437-444.

10
Joseph,
the Husband of Mary

Matthew 1:18–2:23

```
I. HIS EMPLOYMENT
II. HIS ENGAGEMENT
III. HIS EMBARRASSMENT
IV. HIS ENCOURAGEMENT
V. HIS ENLIGHTENMENT
VI. HIS ENJOYMENT
VII. HIS ENNOBLEMENT
```

Joseph was not rich, but he must have been a remarkable man. God would not have chosen a mean man, a miserly man, a moody man, a mediocre man, or a merciless man to be the foster father of His Son. Although we only catch a brief glance of Joseph in the Bible, we see enough to know he was careful, conscientious, concerned, and compassionate—a fitting foster father for Jesus.

I. HIS EMPLOYMENT

Joseph was a village carpenter. He knew what it was like to toil at a workbench and barely make ends meet. We can be sure he was honest in his business dealings and we can be sure he worked hard, but he does not seem to have made much money. We gather that he was poor because when the time came for the presentation of the infant Christ in the temple in Jerusalem, the best offering he and Mary could afford was the smallest and least expensive sacrifice the Mosaic law allowed.

Yet this poor humble laboring man was a prince in his own right. We cannot imagine him boasting about his ancestry, but he could have. He could have said to his friends: "I'm a direct descendant of good King Josiah. I am related to King Hezekiah. My family tree goes back to Solomon. I am of the lineage of David. I am a member of the Hebrew royal family. The blood of princes flows in my veins. If I had my rights, I would be sitting on the throne of David in Jerusalem right now in place of that scoundrel Edomite Herod." (If Joseph had made such boasts, Herod would have had his head.)

Joseph probably was not a braggart, but he was a direct descendant of David. However, the fortunes of the imperial house of David had sunk so low that instead of sitting on a throne in Jerusalem, the rightful heir to that throne was living in a despised Galilean village and laboring for his daily bread at a carpenter's bench. The tools of his trade were a hammer, an adze, and a saw. He made yokes for oxen, doors for houses, handles for plows, and tables and chairs.

Joseph brought his adopted son up to this trade. Significantly the One who had created a hundred million galaxies labored from His youth at creating things for people. Being thus employed, Jesus forever ennobled manual labor and the crafting of useful and beautiful objects for the benefit of one's fellow men.

II. HIS ENGAGEMENT

A young girl in Nazareth caught young Joseph's eye. She was not immaculately conceived, as some say. The Bible does not support any such idea. But she was as perfect as any daughter of Adam's fallen race could be. She was humble and holy, loving and lowly, patient and pure, thoughtful and kind. God had waited for some four thousand years for this particular woman to be born, so we can be sure that she was as near perfection in character, personality, and disposition as a human woman could be.

Young Joseph knew one thing: he wanted to marry Mary. His sun rose and set on her. She was all anyone could ever want in a wife. He was thrilled when his proposal was accepted and the betrothal arrangements were made.

There were two forms of betrothal among the Jews. We do not know which form was used in the case of Mary and Joseph. In one form the agreement was spoken in the presence of witnesses. The vows were confirmed by the pledging of a piece of money (we can be sure any dowry was small in Mary and Joseph's agreement). In the other form the transaction was confirmed in writing.

Either form of betrothal was probably followed by a supper, a benediction, and a statutory cup of wine for the engaged couple. From that moment on, the prospective bride and groom were pledged to be married. Their relationship was as solemn and sacred as the marriage relationship and any breach of it would be regarded as adultery. The engagement could not be dissolved except by a formal divorce. Yet months—sometimes even a year—elapsed between the engagement and the marriage.

Joseph was the happiest man in Nazareth. Mary filled his whole horizon. He was engaged to be married to a princess of the house of David. She was also related to the priesthood— her mother seems to have been a blood relative of Elizabeth, the wife of Zacharias the priest. This engagement was a remarkable event—not that Joseph cared that much about the lineage of Mary. She was going to marry *him!* That was all that mattered. That good, pure-minded, Bible-believing, spiritual, and capable girl was going to marry him!

For Joseph, heaven above was deeper blue; earth around

was deeper green. We can imagine that he whistled while he worked. He sang as he delivered his wares to his customers. Each week he looked forward to seeing her in the synagogue on Saturday. He counted the days and hours to the wedding. He gazed in rapture at the moon. He was going to marry Mary and all was well with the world. He slept with a lock of her hair under his pillow. He dreamed of the day when the two would at last become one.

III. HIS EMBARRASSMENT

Then one day Mary approached him. "I need to see you, Joseph," she said. "Something has happened. I have something to tell you." We can imagine the shock he received when she broke the news: "I'm going to have a baby."

The news was devastating. Joseph was absolutely stunned. He knew he had never touched her in a dishonorable way. If she was going to have a baby, he was not the father.

Joseph could not believe what he was hearing. He could not imagine his pure and spiritually-minded fiancée doing anything wrong. She was not that kind of girl. She said she had not been raped. She had not committed adultery. She had not betrayed him. She was not interested in anyone else; she never had been and never would be. But she *was* going to have a baby. Joseph could not believe Mary was lying to him. He had always believed her honesty and integrity to be above suspicion.

"Well," he must have said at last, "what *is* your explanation?"

"About six months ago," she might have answered, "my cousin Elizabeth's husband Zacharias was visited by the angel Gabriel. He told Zacharias that Elizabeth was going to give birth to a son. Well, since Elizabeth was too old to have a baby, Zacharias did not believe what Gabriel said, so Gabriel smote Zacharias with dumbness. Then, sure enough, Elizabeth became pregnant. That was six months ago and Zacharias is still dumb. The whole incident caused quite a stir in the priestly confraternity."

"What does that have to do with you?"

"I'm coming to that, Joseph. The angel told Zacharias that his son would be a special child, the forerunner of the Messiah."

"I still don't see what that has to do with you."

"It has everything to do with me. A little while ago that same angel visited me."

"Come on, Mary! You never told me that."

"I'm telling you now. The angel Gabriel visited me. He told me I was to become the mother of the Son of God--that God was going to send His Son into the world as a baby and that I was the chosen vehicle for that birth. Gabriel told me that I would be overshadowed by the Holy Ghost, that I would miraculously conceive, and that the Son of God would be born of me. Now, just as the angel said, I'm going to have a baby. I waited until I knew for sure before I told you. What do you think of that?"

Joseph simply did not believe the story. He could not believe that Mary was with child. He could not believe she had been unfaithful to her betrothal vows, but he could not believe her explanation. He didn't know anyone else who would believe the story either. He wondered whether he was dealing with a moral issue or a miraculous issue. Since Mary's explanation was incredible, the issue had to be a moral one.

"You do believe me, don't you, Joseph?" we can hear Mary say.

"I don't know what to believe. I'm going to have to think it over."

"Well, while you think it over, I'm going to visit my cousin Elizabeth. At least she'll believe me."

And so Mary left and Joseph began to think it over. As far as he was concerned, it was going to take a great deal of thinking over. _Pregnant by divine conception indeed!_ he thought. _Who in his right mind will ever believe a story like that?_

IV. HIS ENCOURAGEMENT

Anyone who has suffered a broken engagement will be able to enter into the mind and heart of Joseph. For him there was deep, deep sorrow and a gnawing anguish of soul. There was a sense of shock and disbelief. Perhaps there were sudden surges of outright anger and resentment. But most of all, there was the nagging ache of a broken heart.

The more Joseph thought over Mary's story, the more it became evident to him that for his own protection under the stern Mosaic law, he would have to break the engagement. The provisions of that law added a new dimension of horror to his agony. For a single girl to become pregnant, especially when betrothed, was a capital offense. The law demanded the death penalty for the guilty parties. Joseph would have to accuse Mary publicly and go on the witness stand to denounce her. Worst of all, when the death sentence was passed he would have to cast the first stone.

He could never do that, but he couldn't marry her now—that would be tantamount to admitting his own guilt. Besides, Mary had betrayed him. How else could her condition be explained? He couldn't believe her story about angelic visitations and a virgin birth. She must be living in a dream world, a world of fantasy and wishful thinking and make-believe.

On the other hand, Mary had spoken with candor and she had always exhibited a stainless character before. Moreover she had rushed right off to Elizabeth of all people. Elizabeth's husband was a priest and would be the first to sit in judgment on an adulteress. Surely Mary's visit to Elizabeth was profoundly significant. If Mary were guilty of immoral conduct, the last place she would go would be Judea, where the laws were more rigidly enforced. The last place she would go would be the house of a priest who would be duty-bound to report her.

So a disconsolate Joseph thought the situation over as he wandered the streets of Nazareth. Every corner, every tree, every hill, and every dale reminded him of her. The place was haunted now by a ghost. Mary was gone and Nazareth was a place without a soul. His hometown had suddenly become a city of sepulchers, the grave of all his hopes.

The wind in the trees reminded him of the sound of Mary's voice blithely singing the Psalms of their great ancestor David. The village fountain where the girls gathered and chatted brought back memories. The synagogue was a place of torture. On the sabbath Mary's place was empty now. He could only sit and stare at it sadly, choking back his tears. Joseph felt like abandoning the synagogue and its services altogether.

The mental torture continued until one day, we can imagine, he flung down his hammer and strode out of the carpenter's shop. He went out of the town and up the hill to the place, perchance, where years later the villagers would seek to throw Jesus to His death. There Joseph halted and, frightened, drew back from the drop. He sank down to the ground and wept bitter tears. He had to come to a decision one way or another. In his agony he decided to break the engagement privately and let matters take their course. Exhausted, but glad that some decision, however wretched, had been made, he fell asleep.

Suddenly his sleep was ablaze with light. Scripture tells us the angel of the Lord appeared—not just Gabriel, but the Jehovah angel. The words of the angel rang in his soul: "Joseph, thou son of David, fear not to take unto thee Mary thy wife: for that which is conceived in her is of the Holy Ghost. And she shall bring forth a son, and thou shalt call his name JESUS: for he shall save his people from their sins (Matthew 1:20-21).

The storm clouds rolled away and the sun broke through again. The words of the prophet Isaiah came to Joseph's mind: "Behold, a virgin shall be with child, and shall bring forth a son, and they shall call his name Emmanuel, which being interpreted is, God with us" (Matthew 1:23). Within an hour, we can imagine, Joseph was running as fast as his legs could carry him to Judea. From then on his steps would be ordered of the Lord.

V. HIS ENLIGHTENMENT

After Mary and Joseph were married, a decree came from Caesar Augustus. They were to go back to the city of their birth to be enrolled for taxation purposes. Mary was approaching the time of her confinement, but the word of the caesar had to be obeyed. In the providence of God, the decree meant that in keeping with an ancient prophecy the holy child would be born in Bethlehem. Perhaps the couple were glad to leave Nazareth. Indeed it took a special divine revelation to bring them back to Nazareth (Matthew 2:19-23).

The journey from Nazareth to Bethlehem must have taken at least three days. Probably Mary and Joseph followed the route along the eastern bank of the Jordan to avoid going through hostile Samaria. As they approached the heights of Bethlehem, they could see one of Herod's frowning castles perched on the highest hill southeast of Bethlehem. On they went until the mountain ridges of Tekoa came into view. East of the travelers lay the sullen waters of the Dead Sea. To the west the road wound away to Hebron. To the north was undulating countryside behind which Jerusalem was hidden. And in front of them at last was Bethlehem.

Mary must have been exhausted and Joseph not a little anxious to get her settled for the night, for her time had come. But alas there was no room in the inn and thus the Son of God came from the mansions of glory, from the ivory palaces of Heaven, to a wayside cattle shed. We can be sure, however, that Joseph did what he could to clean up the worst of the filth. He found a manger and filled it with straw and hay so that the newborn babe might have a clean and comfortable bed.

The shepherds came and the angels sang. Joseph moved his family into a more convenient place and the wise men came with their timely gifts. Then the angel of the Lord appeared again and said to Joseph, "Arise, and take the young child and his mother, and flee into Egypt, and be thou there until I bring thee word: for Herod will seek the young child to destroy him"

(Matthew 2:13). That child was Lord and Creator of the universe—He could have called ten thousand angels to stop Herod and his men of war dead in their tracks. Instead He fled to Egypt! God had His own timetable for bringing judgment on Herod.

Joseph and his family stayed in Egypt until the death of Herod. And a terrible death it was. The cup of Herod's crimes was full and his torments and terrors came. He was haunted by visions of a rival to the throne and he sacrificed thousands of innocent people to that fear, including his favorite wife and various sons. He died demented of a dreadful disease that devoured his body. According to Edersheim the visit of the Magi took place in February. In March Herod rounded up all the rabbis he could lay his hands on, locked them up, and left orders for them to be executed on the day of his death. At the end of March or beginning of April he murdered his son Antipater and Herod himself was dead five days later.

He was succeeded by his son Archelaus, who spent the night of his father's death carousing and rioting with his friends. One of his first acts as king was to massacre three thousand Jews within the sacred precincts of the temple. Vile as his father had been, Archelaus was worse. He surpassed him in cruelty, oppression, opulence, pride, and sensuality.

Soon after the death of Herod, Joseph returned to Palestine. It seems he wanted to settle in Bethlehem, a proper setting for great David's greater Son, but Joseph was directed to go back to Galilee and thus Jesus grew up in Nazareth.

VI. HIS ENJOYMENT

What greater joy could any man on earth have had than the joy of being foster father to Jesus, the Son of the living God? Christ's presence in Joseph's humble home was a benediction.

Jesus grew up giving Joseph the courtesy title of "father." When Mary reprimanded Him for tarrying in the temple on the occasion of His first Jerusalem Passover, she said, "*Thy father* and I have sought thee sorrowing" (Luke 2:48, italics added). So Joseph parented Jesus. Joseph surrounded Him with love and kindness and counsel and all the necessities of life. And Jesus responded by being the only absolutely perfect child and teenager who ever blessed a human home.

We can imagine how Joseph delighted in the willing, cheerful obedience of Jesus to every command; in His loving, joyful, peaceable disposition; in His uniformly excellent grades at school; in His enjoyment of the Word of God; and in His wisdom and universal popularity. There never was such a boy in all this world, and it was Joseph's privilege to provide the setting for that jewel to be displayed. A humble setting it was: a small, primitive, but comfortable house and a nearby carpenter's shop.

Joseph must have felt an inner glow when the neighbors were impressed. One of them would ask, "How's that boy Jesus doing at school?" And Joseph could reply, "Jesus? He's a straight-A student. He has already memorized the Pentateuch and mops up languages like a sponge." Another neighbor would add to the pleasure: "I say, Joseph, your son Jesus was at our place the other day. He brought my wife some flowers from the field to cheer her sickroom. She says it was a tonic just to have Him visit."

So Joseph played the part of protector, provider, and parent to the Son of the living God, and he enjoyed every minute of it.

VII. HIS ENNOBLEMENT

We will not find this Joseph in *Who's Who in the World*, but we can be quite sure that his name is written down in the book of God's kingdom. When the roll of that kingdom's great ones is called, we will hear the name of Joseph. Yes indeed, and we will also hear the part of the story that is not recorded in the Bible.

11
Pilate,
the Judge of Jesus

John 19:19

I. A PEOPLE HE DESPISED

II. A PLACE HE DERIDED

III. A PERSON HE DISOWNED

IV. A PRINCE HE DENIED

When Pontius Pilate left Rome for Palestine, the emperor Tiberius gave him a special gold ring. It identified Pilate as an *amicus Caesaris,* "friend of the caesar." To keep that ring, as much as for any other reason, Pilate allowed Christ, a man he knew was innocent, to be crucified.

Pilate's ancestors were Roman nobles of the equestrian order. He had served a tour of duty in Syria as an administrative military tribune with the Twelfth Legion and had earned the reputation of being a tough commander. His wife, Claudia Procula, is said to have been the granddaughter of Caesar Augustus, so Pilate had the highest connections in Rome.

As procurator of Judea, Pilate carried a heavy responsibility. Judea was the capital of the seven million Jews who lived in the Roman empire—7 percent of its entire population.

Moreover Judea commanded the trade routes and lines of communication between Syria and Egypt. Judea was also important because it was the only outpost preventing Parthia from moving in and blocking Roman access to Egypt. Rome depended on Egypt for her grain supply, so Egypt itself could not be allowed to fall into hostile hands either. And the ships that carried their precious cargoes of wheat to Rome must never be endangered. So the governorship of Judea was a trust of some magnitude.

Pilate was not going to allow some local messiah to imperil his position as friend of the caesar and guardian of Rome's Egyptian gate, so he caved in to political expediency. If he let Jesus go, he would incur the wrath of the Sanhedrin. If he let Jesus go, he would in effect be endorsing Christ's claim to be a king—the King of the Jews.

Having rejected the claims of Christ against the advice of his wife and the instinct of his own soul, having signed the death warrant that consigned Jesus to a particularly cruel and horrible death, and having uselessly washed his hands of the whole business, Pilate gave Jesus a title. As was customary in the case of a public execution, the governor wrote a placard naming both the criminal and the crime. Much to the annoyance of the Jews, Pilate wrote: "JESUS OF NAZARETH THE KING OF THE JEWS" (John 19:19). "This title," John recalled, "then read many of the Jews: for the place where Jesus was crucified was nigh to the city: and it was written in Hebrew, and Greek, and Latin" (19:20). The placard was written in Latin, the language of government; in Greek, the language of culture; and in Hebrew, the language of religion. The title was written in all three languages so that all the world could read and consider both the Christ and His claims.

Doubtless Pilate wrote the title tongue-in-cheek. He was annoyed at the Jews for pushing this case off on him. He knew perfectly well that at the bottom of their maneuvering was a deep-seated envy of Jesus of Nazareth. Pilate knew from his spies scattered throughout the country that Jesus was a good man and that He posed no threat to Roman rule. Had He not said, "Render to Caesar the things that are Caesar's, and to God the things that are God's" (Mark 12:17)? At His trial He had conducted Himself with extraordinary self-control and poise. Pilate had been impressed. Pilate knew He was innocent of the charges brought against Him. Jesus confessed to be a King but at once declared that His kingdom was not of this world. He claimed to have come from another world altogether, and Pilate more than half believed Him and was more than a little afraid of Him.

So to get even with the Jews for the annoyance, inconvenience, embarrassment, and anxiety they had caused him, Pilate wrote: "Jesus of Nazareth the King of the Jews." And he would not change the wording. "What I have written I have written," he said (John 19:22).

The placard that Pilate wrote and had nailed to Christ's cross was more significant than he realized. The title revealed a people Pilate despised, a place he derided, a person he disowned, and a prince he denied.

I. A PEOPLE HE DESPISED
"Jesus of Nazareth the King of the JEWS"

The Jews were much older than the Romans. Before Pompey marched into Jerusalem, the Jews were a great people. When the Romans were still bearded barbarians, the Jews were already a great people. Before the story of Romulus and Remus and the she-wolf was circulated, the Jews were a great people.

Before Alexander the Great was crowned king of Macedonia in 336 B.C., the Jews were a great people. Before the Athenians began building the Parthenon in 447 B.C., the Jews were a great people. Before Xerxes invaded Greece, before Cyrus the Persian conquered Babylon, before Nebuchadnezzar rose to power, before the Phoenicians founded Carthage, before the Assyrians forged their cruel empire, before Ramses the Great began construction of the temple of Abu Simbel—the

Jews were already a great people. Their roots and their history go far back—back before Hammurabi of Babylon hammered out his legal code, back before the Hyksos kings subdued Egypt. When the Bronze Age was coming to flower in Egypt, the Jews were a people to be reckoned with in this world.

Perhaps Pilate did not know his history book, but the Jews, a people he despised, were a people not to be despised. They had a legal code greater than Rome's. They had a religion greater—far greater—than Rome's. Even in Pilate's day the Jews were the world's bankers. But Pilate despised the Jews because Rome measured a man by his might and the Jews were not famous as fighters.

In sizing up the Jews, however, Pilate was ignoring the wars of the Maccabees. And before the century was over, the Jews would teach Rome a lesson it would not soon forget. To quell the Jewish revolt, the Romans were forced to assemble an army of eighty thousand men. Alexander the Great had carved out his vast empire with thirty-two thousand men. Julius Caesar needed only twenty-five thousand soldiers to conquer Gaul and invade Britain. To fight the Jews, however, Titus was forced to mobilize ten thousand cavalrymen and seventy thousand infantrymen, and even against those odds the Jews kept the Romans at bay for four long years. In the end the Romans won, not because of greater skill but because of greater numbers. After the Romans conquered Jerusalem, they still had to subdue Masada. And the Jews led by Bar Kokhba tried to resist Rome again in A.D. 135.

The Jews would outlast Pilate, the caesar he served, and the empire he represented. When the Huns and Goths and Vandals at last descended on Rome, the Jews were still a mighty people. They are a mighty people today. Every nation or empire that has ever turned its hand against the Jews has in the end found itself fighting against God.

But Pilate despised this people. He wrote his contempt into the title he made for the cross: "Jesus of Nazareth the King of the *Jews*." To him the title was ludicrous. Everybody knew the Jews had no king. The king who reigned over them was Herod. And the king who ruled over Herod was a Roman. Pilate thought of the Jews as moneylenders. He thought of them as religious fanatics. He thought of greedy men like Annas and guileful men like Caiaphas. The idea that the Jews should have a king struck him as ridiculous.

II. A PLACE HE DERIDED
"Jesus of NAZARETH the King of the Jews"

Nazareth! Even the Jews regarded this Galilean town with a measure of contempt. They despised Galileans because they were of mixed blood; because so many Gentiles lived in Galilee; and because its chief city was Tiberius, doubly unclean since it was named after a despised emperor and it was built on the site of an old graveyard. The Jews despised Galileans because they were "unlearned and ignorant men" (Acts 4:13) and because they spoke the native Aramaic with a thick, north-country accent.

The Jews despised Nazareth even more. "Can there any good thing come out of Nazareth?" asked Nathanael when Philip told him he had found the Messiah, a man named Jesus of Nazareth (John 1:45-46). Pilate had been governor of Judea long enough to know how much Nazareth was despised by the Jews. "Jesus of *Nazareth*," he wrote, hoping to annoy the Jews still further. If the accused had been Jesus of Rome, Jesus of Athens, Jesus of Carthage, or even Jesus of Jerusalem, Pilate may have paid more heed to the case. For a Jesus of Nazareth to claim kingship struck Pilate as absurd.

Nazareth wasn't much of a place by worldly standards. We can imagine there were cypress trees reaching toward the sky, terraces of fig and olive trees, poor homes, a fountain supplying the town's only water, a market, and a carpenter's shop. With a clientele of struggling farmers and agricultural workers, the carpenter was paid once a year at harvest time in produce and grain.

Jesus, His mother, Joseph, and His half brothers and sisters would have lived in a room above a cave where a donkey was kept. The room would have been virtually bare of furniture. Bedding mats would have been rolled up and tucked away in a corner. Such cramped quarters were typical of Nazareth.

Although Nazareth was not in his province, Pilate doubtless knew all there was to know about the place. In a way the town was significant as a dividing line. To its south were Jerusalem and Judea and Old Testament religious norms. To the north was upper Galilee. To go from Judea to Galilee was almost to turn one's back on the Old Testament world. Galilee was crossed by the great north-south military roads and by the east-west caravan routes. Galilee was an international corridor and Nazareth was its gateway.

The sophisticated Judeans spoke the name of Nazareth with a sneer and Pilate would have preferred Caesarea any time. Sophisticated Caesarea was a transplant of Rome. Caesarea had a fine harbor where Roman warships could drop anchor. It had magnificent theaters, a hippodrome, a marble temple, and the great palace of Herod. Pilate chuckled as he wrote *Nazareth* on the sign. It was a place to be derided.

III. A PERSON HE DISOWNED
"JESUS of Nazareth the King of the Jews"

Jesus was a common name among the Jews of Pilate's day. The name had its roots in the Hebrew for Joshua, pronounced *Yeshua*. Whether Pilate knew or appreciated the meaning of the name is questionable. *Jesus* means "Jehovah the Savior." To the Christian, Jesus is the sweetest name on earth. To Pilate it was the name of just another Jew. Ultimately Pilate had to choose between two names: Jesus and Tiberius—the King of the Jews or the emperor of Rome.

Caesar Tiberius was the adopted stepson of Caesar Augustus. In the early days of his reign, Tiberius had the reputation of being an able soldier and administrator. But he had a vicious streak in him and before long he was thoroughly detested in Rome, not only for his cruelties but also for his abominable vices. He retired to the island of Capri and abandoned himself to all forms of lust. When he finally died, there was such rejoicing in Rome that people ran about shouting, "To the Tiber with Tiberius!" Others offered prayers to the infernal gods to give him no room below except among the damned. To this disgusting and debauched individual Pilate owed his promotion. There was little doubt in Pilate's mind about whether he would choose the caesar or the Christ. Pilate would choose the caesar.

Everything Pilate had ever heard about Jesus was extraordinary and we can be sure nothing happened in the provinces that wasn't known in Pilate's palace. "He goes about doing good," his spies would tell him. "He performs astounding miracles. Herod Antipas is dying to see one of them. Jesus heals sick people. He casts out evil spirits. He feeds the hungry. He has even cleansed lepers and raised the dead. Many of the common people take His name to be prophetic and consider Him to be their Savior."

When face to face with Jesus, Pilate felt the awesome goodness and power of the man. Pilate had never ever met a man like Him before. Indeed the procurator seems to have been superstitious about Jesus, but he banished his superstitious fears and decided that Jesus was just another Jew—a remarkable one, but just a Jew. Thus when Pilate sat down to write the title for the cross, he wrote the name of Jesus without any real understanding of the significance of that name.

It is _the saving name._ When Joseph was trying to make up his mind what to do about Mary, he had a visit from an angel who set his mind at rest. The angel told him that the child about to be born was indeed the very Son of God, then added, "Thou shalt call his name JESUS: for he shall save his people from their sins" (Matthew 1:21). The name was not an everyday name; it embodied an eternal truth. Jesus is the Savior of His people.

"Neither is there salvation in any other," Peter bluntly told the Sanhedrin, who were responsible for the murder of the Messiah. They were equally responsible for efforts to hush up stories about the resurrection and attempts to stop the spread of the gospel. Peter added, "There is none other name under heaven given among men, whereby we must be saved" (Acts 4:12).

Years later when the apostle Paul was a prisoner in Rome, he sent some sound advice to the church at Colosse: "Whatsoever ye do in word or deed," he wrote, "do all in the name of the Lord Jesus" (Colossians 3:17). We cannot go far wrong when His name governs our character, conduct, and conversation. The name of Jesus is *the sanctifying name.* When it is the dominant color on the canvas of one's life, His name sets a very high standard indeed. We should take Paul's advice and echo the words of hymnist James Rowe:

> Be like Jesus—this my song—
> In the home and in the throng;
> Be like Jesus all day long!
> I would be like Jesus.

Pilate asked, "What is truth?" when Truth was staring him in the face (John 18:38). Jesus had said just the day before, "I am the...truth" (14:6). Face to face with Truth incarnate, Pilate sold Him for a lie. The procurator persuaded himself that it was in his own best interest to stay in the good graces of Caiaphas and his crowd and to do nothing that the suspicious old tyrant back in Rome might interpret as treason. So Pilate signed a death warrant and wrote a title. In effect it said, "This is Jesus ...just another Jew."

IV. A PRINCE HE DENIED
"Jesus of Nazareth the KING of the Jews"

When Pilate sent Jesus to Herod Antipas, Herod arrayed Him in mocking purple. Herod had the right idea. Pilate went further. He let his soldiers crown this King of the Jews with a crown of thorns. Would Pilate himself *crown* Him or *crucify* Him? Would he dismiss all charges against this innocent man or would he sign the most infamous death warrant in history? Pilate crucified Him and the same day made friends with Herod Antipas. The man who mocked Christ and the man who murdered Christ shook hands that day.

Contrary to all appearances, the man on the center cross was indeed the King of the Jews. But He was more than that—much more. In the book of Revelation He is called King of kings and Lord of lords!

Pilate soon had an inkling that He was a Prince indeed. A crucified man often lingered on for days in his death agony, but the Sanhedrin urged Pilate to hasten the end of the current victims because of the approaching Passover. Pilate cooperated, ordering that the victims' legs be broken. Then the centurion came in to report that Jesus was dead—not from crucifixion, not from further action ordered by Pilate, but by a sovereign act of His will. He had simply dismissed His spirit and died. Other phenomena had occurred. A supernatural darkness had descended on the country from the sixth to the ninth hour. The temple veil had been torn asunder in some mysterious way. An earthquake had shaken the ground. Reports began to come in from all over the country that graves and sepulchers had burst open.

Three days later Pilate was faced with the news that the tomb was empty and the man he had murdered was alive, back from the dead. At the same time the open graves had discharged their dead. As Matthew 27:52-53 records, "Many bodies of the saints which slept arose, And came out of the graves after his resurrection, and went into the holy city, and appeared unto many."

Jesus was more than the King of the Jews. The centurion ventured his own opinion: "This," he said at the cross, "was the Son of God" (Matthew 27:54). Perhaps he was bold enough to repeat those words to Pilate. But Pilate had denied Him. To the end of his days he would carry with him the memory of eyes that had looked into his and read his very soul. Pilate's assessment of Jesus had been wrong. If only he could rewrite that title! If only he had never written it at all! He should have crowned Him. Perhaps when, as one tradition tells us, he was a lonely outcast banished from power, he belatedly did crown Him as King of his own life.

12
Antichrist,
the Beast of the Apocalypse

Revelation 13,17

I. HIS PARENTAGE

II. HIS PROPHET

III. HIS POLICY

IV. HIS PERSECUTION

V. HIS PARALYSIS

VI. HIS PUNISHMENT

He is known by many names. He is called the Assyrian, the lawless one, the man of sin, the son of perdition, the little horn, and the prince. We often call him the antichrist. In the Apocalypse he is usually called the beast.

The antichrist has been foreshadowed in history time and time again. *Cain* was the first in a long series of men who by their wicked works and willful ways prefigured him. Cain went out from the presence of the Lord a marked man. Having refused to become a pilgrim and a stranger on the earth, he became instead a fugitive and a vagabond. He laid the foundations of a thriving and energetic civilization that became so utterly godless and vile that it had to be divinely overthrown by the waters of the flood.

Nimrod was another type of the antichrist. His name means "the rebel." He determined to build a society to suit himself. It was to be a humanistic and rebellious kingdom. Three times the words "Let us" occur in the story of the tower Nimrod's civilization built. All the emphasis was on man. "Let us make us a name," they said (Genesis 11:4). Nimrod's society was to be a new-age civilization, a united-nations organization, a world federation of nations—with God left out. There was to be a one-world *sovereignty* symbolized by the city, a one-world *society* symbolized by the common language, and a one-world *sanctuary* symbolized by the tower. And Nimrod, the great rebel himself, would preside over it all. Babylon was to be center of his empire and idolatry was to be its religion.

One of the strongest types of the antichrist in history and Biblical revelation was *Antiochus Epiphanes.* This Syrian tyrant conquered Jerusalem in 168 B.C. and massacred the worshipers in the temple. He issued a decree that everyone had to join a universal religion and obey universal laws—or face the death penalty. He seized the Jewish temple and consecrated it to Jupiter (Zeus). Antiochus identified himself with this pagan god and ordered everyone to worship him. He also ordered an immediate cessation of all Jewish sacrifices and suspended all Jewish religious observances. He destroyed all the copies of the Scriptures he could find. He replaced the annual feast of tabernacles with a feast dedicated to Bacchus. Antiochus built an idol altar over the brazen altar in the temple court. In the temple itself he installed an image of Zeus, the thunderer of Olympus. Antiochus sacrificed a sow on the altar, made broth of its flesh, and sprinkled the broth all over the temple. He perverted the youth of the city and taught them vile practices. He massacred thousands of Jews, although there were numerous apostate Jews who admired and followed him. Antiochus was one of Satan's forerunners of the coming antichrist.

There have been other men in the long course of history who have staged dress rehearsals for the coming of the antichrist. The devilish *Nero,* for example, staged a fearful persecution of the Christian church. *Napoleon,* who aimed to resurrect the old Roman empire and conquer Palestine, used the Roman Catholic Church as a pawn in much the same way the antichrist will. *Hitler* sought to bring Europe under his control, and his holocaust against the Jews was a precursor of the coming great tribulation.

The Bible tells us many things about the actual antichrist. It reveals his parentage, his prophet, his policy, his persecution, his paralysis, and his punishment.

I. HIS PARENTAGE

In Revelation 12 the great red dragon appears in Heaven. He has seven heads and ten horns and is easily identified as the devil. We see his malice toward the nation of Israel and his thwarted effort to destroy the man-child, the Lord Jesus, at His birth.

In Revelation 13 we see "a beast rise up out of the sea" (13:1). It too has seven heads and ten horns. We read about this beast again in Revelation 17, which emphasizes the seven heads and ten horns and provides the additional information that he is "a scarlet coloured beast" (17:3).

The great red dragon is Satan and the scarlet-colored beast is the antichrist. The beast betrays his parentage, for he looks and acts like the great red dragon. In other words, the father of the beast is the devil himself.

Revelation 17 gives us more information about the beast. He is to be killed and brought back to life again, so he has two comings. When he comes the first time, he rises out of the sea. In other words, the beast is an ordinary human being who rises out of the sea of the nations and out of *the* sea, namely the Mediterranean world. He will probably be a Roman because he is identified with the little horn of Daniel 7.

Some people think that the beast will be only part human, that he will actually be fathered by Satan. Since Jesus said concerning Judas, "Have not I chosen you twelve, and one of you is a devil?" (John 6:70) some assume that both Judas and the antichrist are of Satanic origin. Since Jesus called Judas "the son of perdition" (John 17:12) and this title is only used elsewhere for the antichrist (2 Thessalonians 2:3), some surmise that Judas and the antichrist are the same individual. People who make this assumption point to Acts 1:25, which says that Judas, after he hanged himself, went "to his own place." They speculate that Judas is presently being groomed in the underworld to come back as the antichrist.

More likely the beast out of the sea will be a Gentile—a Roman who will revive the old empire. He will rule as the last of the caesars. He will also be the final heir to Nebuchadnezzar's lordship of the world. The antichrist, at his first coming, will be a very attractive, dynamic, clever individual who will charm and fascinate the nations. Probably he will sell himself to the devil, as Hitler did. The antichrist will be taught and led by principalities and powers and rulers of this world's darkness (see Ephesians 6:12).

Revelation 17 tells us he will be killed, but it does not tell us how. Perhaps the antichrist will be slain when God's two witnesses (Revelation 11) and Satan's two representatives (the beast and the false prophet) wage war against each other. That war will be a battle of miracles similar to that which took place in Egypt when Moses and Aaron confronted the pharaoh's two false prophets.

God will permit Satan to bring the antichrist back to life again. Thereafter he will be known not as "the beast out of the sea" (Revelation 13:1-4) but as "the beast out of the bottomless pit" (11:7; 17:8-11). From this point on he will be a supernatural being and will be universally worshiped. The antichrist will be Satan incarnate, the visible expression of the invisible devil and the vehicle through whom Satan will try to accomplish his purposes for this planet.

II. HIS PROPHET

Revelation 13 chronicles the coming of two beasts. The first rises out of the sea and is therefore a Gentile. The second comes up out of the earth and is therefore a Jew because the earth stands in contrast to the sea in Old Testament typology and symbolism. The second beast will be subordinate to the first one, but they will be soul twins. The second beast looks like a lamb, but speaks like a dragon. Thus he too betrays his Satanic origin. He is called "the false prophet" (Revelation 16:13) and he will exercise all the power of the first beast. The false prophet will be the first beast's high priest and spokesman. The false prophet will persuade the world that the first beast is the long-awaited messiah and that the world's interests lie in submitting to him.

The Lord Jesus warned that as the last days begin to dawn, numerous false prophets will arise and deceive many (Matthew 24:11). All the world's false religions have been founded by false prophets. The church has had its false prophets too. Today false cults in Christendom deceive millions. But these false prophets are simply part of Satan's general attack on the Christian faith. He is the father of lies, and deception is the idiom of his language. He uses false religions to keep lost people lost. Satan is not against religion; he is all for it; he invented most of it.

However a false prophet of quite a different kind is still to come. He will be known as *the* false prophet. He will come with deceit and lying wonders and will wield all the power and authority of his master, the antichrist. The false prophet will be a golden-tongued orator and will appear to be harmless. Satan will enable him to speak as one inspired and only those enlightened by the Holy Spirit will be able to withstand his persuasive eloquence. The false prophet will make wickedness seem right. His miracles will dazzle and deceive. Except for those whose names are written in the Lamb's book of life, the human race will fall for him and follow him. The false prophet will lead them to the antichrist, the antichrist will lead them to Satan, and Satan will lead them to Hell.

The only safeguard for the human race will be the Word of God. But since men will long since have abandoned that for the countless false religions and philosophies abroad in the world, the false prophet will persuade men that the antichrist is their long-sought savior.

III. HIS POLICY

When the antichrist first appears, he will be just a "little horn" (Daniel 7:7-8,16-26)—that is, he will not have a great deal of power. But he will be the consummate master of craft and cunning. He will arise somewhere in southern Europe, probably in Rome, and will be given a seat in the councils of the ten kings, the European leaders who control a shadow Roman empire. He will make short work of three of them and then control all ten of them.

The details in Scripture are sketchy, but we do know from Revelation 17 that the antichrist will make common cause with the Roman Catholic Church. The Vatican will think it can control him, but it will soon discover that it has allied itself to a tiger. The antichrist will use this religious system to gain the upper hand in Europe and in all countries where Catholicism is entrenched. The Vatican will think it can use this "little horn" to get back its lost power and authority in the world, but as soon as the antichrist has made the ten kings subservient to his will, he will turn on the ecclesiastical system and tear it to pieces. The ten kings themselves will gleefully fall upon the enormous wealth and riches of the Roman Catholic Church and divide the spoils among themselves.

As soon as the antichrist is securely enthroned as the ruler of Europe and the revived Roman empire, he will act swiftly to expand his power. We are not told specifically what part the United States and the western hemisphere will play in all this. The "old lion" (the European powers—Isaiah 60:9; Ezekiel

38:13) will be loose. The lands of the Americas are the young lions spawned centuries ago by the old lion. Perhaps the antichrist will simply pull the economic rug out from beneath the United States and thus bankrupt the United States, Canada, and Latin America. Then he may form a new Atlantic alliance in which the countries of the western hemisphere take orders from Rome. Once he has the western world at his command, the antichrist will prepare to satisfy larger ambitions, for his goal is to rule the world.

The rule of the world was granted in principle to Nebuchadnezzar, with whom the "times of the Gentiles" began (Luke 21:24). He only ruled a tithe of the whole. His successors in the prophetic world were the leaders of Medo-Persia, Greece, and Rome, but none of these men ruled the whole world. With the revival of the Roman empire and the formation of the new Atlantic alliance, the way will be clear for the antichrist to pursue his plans for a truly global empire. All the economic, industrial, and military might of the West will be at his disposal and he will be ready to further his schemes.

The antichrist will sign a treaty with Israel—an agreement with Hell (Isaiah 28:15). This seven-year treaty will activate the seventieth and final "week" of seven years still hanging in abeyance (see Daniel 9 for the vision of the seventy weeks). Under the terms of this treaty the antichrist apparently will guarantee Israel's security and authorize them to rebuild their temple. He will allow that temple to be built for a reason.

We can imagine the howl of rage that will come from the Muslim world when the Jews start to rebuild their temple on its ancient site. But the Muslims will be powerless. They fear that at the slightest hint of opposition the antichrist will want to occupy all Arab territory down to the Euphrates. He will not want a huddle of quarrelsome Middle East Arab states to spoil his global plans. He will want to get rid of Islam if it looms as an obstacle to the accomplishment of his ultimate goals.

So the Islamic powers will appeal to Russia, which will be looking for a chance to reassert itself as a world superpower.

Russia will seize this invitation to move into the Middle East. Ezekiel 38 seems to indicate that a united Germany will join Russia and the Islamic states in a massive antisemitic alliance. Russia and its allies will move swiftly and the combined armies will cross the frontier into Israel. Then God will act. The terrible disasters spoken of in Ezekiel 38–39 will overtake the invading powers, and their armies will be virtually annihilated. Their homelands will also be visited by divine judgment. Suddenly Russia, Germany, and the Islamic powers will no longer exist.

The way will thus be open for the antichrist to achieve his goal of global sovereignty. Before the rest of the world can recover from the astounding news that Russia and her allies have been destroyed, the armies of the antichrist will occupy their territories. He will issue an ultimatum to the eastern nations: Join me—or else. They will say: "Who is like unto the beast? who is able to make war with him?" (Revelation 13:4)

The eastern nations will quickly submit to the all-conquering antichrist, who will now have three capitals: *Rome,* his political capital; *Jerusalem,* his religious capital; and rebuilt *Babylon,* his economic capital. He will have achieved the goal of hundreds of would-be world conquerors. He will rule the whole world.

IV. HIS PERSECUTION

Having no more use for the Jews, the antichrist will tear off the mask of friendship and show his real face. He will seize the rebuilt temple in Jerusalem and put an image of himself in the temple. The false prophet will give the image life and endow it with power to destroy those who refuse to worship it.

The antichrist will order a test of allegiance: People will be required to prove their loyalty to the new world order by receiving the antichrist's mark on their right hands or on their foreheads. Without that mark no one will be able to buy or sell. A total economic boycott of those not wearing this badge will be globally enforced. A little boy will not even be able to buy an ice cream cone without the mark.

"The mark of the beast" (Revelation 16:2; 19:20) will be related to the name of the beast. Revelation 13:17-18 tells us "the number of his name." In Hebrew and Greek every letter is also a number, so every word is not only a collection of letters but also a collection of numbers. Thus every word has a numerical value. The Greek letters that make up the name of Jesus add up to 888. The numerical value of the antichrist's name, when it is finally revealed, will be 666.

Those with a Judeo-Christian background, those who have been converted by the preaching of the 144,000, and those who fear God more than they fear man will be persecuted. Those who refuse to wear the mark of the beast will pay the price. Satan will launch his most determined effort to rid the world of all lingering traces of the true and living God. The resulting holocaust will make the horror camps of the Nazis look like a Sunday school picnic.

But God will not abdicate the throne. Not for one moment will He surrender His sovereignty. The antichrist's day of reckoning will come.

V. HIS PARALYSIS

Even as the antichrist rides the crest of his power, things will begin to go wrong. The vials of God's wrath will be outpoured. The first four vials will be aimed at the antichrist's power structure on the planet. Under the hammer blows of Heaven he will lose his grip and his might will begin to ebb away.

The eastern half of the antichrist's empire, the nations east of the Euphrates, will break away. (The Euphrates has always been the dividing line between East and West.) A new eastern coalition will be thrown together and the "kings of the east" will mobilize against him (Revelation 16:12). Japanese technology will be married to Chinese manpower. The great eastern hordes will rally to the rebel cause. The united armies of the East will march westward, cross the Euphrates, and deploy on the plains of Megiddo. The antichrist will mobilize the West, and the vast armies of East and West will face each other, determined to decide once and for all who is going to rule the world. The stage will be set for the battle of Armageddon.

VI. HIS PUNISHMENT

Before the battle can begin, there will be an invasion from outer space: Jesus will come again! This time He will be backed by the armies of Heaven. The church will be there in all its glory. All the Lord's might and majesty will be revealed. The sword will go forth from His mouth and the conflict will be over. The armies of earth will be swept away, and the antichrist and his false prophet will stand alone gazing at an enormous field strewn with dead bodies.

The judgment of the antichrist and the false prophet will be swift and sure. They will be seized and flung headlong into the lake of fire, and the smoke of their torment will rise up on high. The antichrist's rickety empire will be quickly dismembered. The survivors—Jew and Gentile alike—of the years of famine, pestilence, earthquake, persecution, and war will be summoned to the valley of Jehoshaphat. There, near the site of Gethsemane, the Lord Himself will separate the sheep from the goats. The world will be fully cleansed of all those who wear the mark of the beast, of all those who joined the great conspiracy. Those who pass judgment will be regenerated and sent to pioneer the millennial kingdom in the name of Christ. But that's another story!